Also by Alain Touraine
*The May Movement: Revolt and Reform*

# THE
# POST-INDUSTRIAL
# SOCIETY

# THE POST-INDUSTRIAL SOCIETY
Tomorrow's Social History: Classes, Conflicts and Culture in the Programmed Society

**ALAIN TOURAINE**

*Translated by Leonard F. X. Mayhew*

**RANDOM HOUSE**  *New York*

# Acknowledgments

The essential elements of the texts which make up this book are original. Some of them are entirely so. Others are based on published articles which have been so profoundly transformed that it seemed necessary to change even their titles.

I must nevertheless cite the origin of the articles which have served as points of departure for several chapters of this book, and I thank the publishers and directors of the periodicals or collections for their permission to use them.

The Introduction, "The Programmed Society and its Sociology," has not been published before.

The first chapter is a new version of the article "Anciennes et nouvelles classes sociales," which appeared in the collection *Perspectives de la sociologie contemporaine,* published in honor of Georges Gurvitch under the direction of Georges Balandier, Paris, P.U.F., 1968. This text was written in 1965.

The next chapter has two parts. The first has not been published before. The second, which bears on international analysis of the student movements, was published in *Information sur les sciences sociales,* Paris, Conseil international des sciences sociales, April 1969. This text was written in December 1968.

The third chapter is a profoundly modified version of the article "L'entreprise: rationalisation et politique," published in a special number of *Economie appliquée*, directed by François Perroux and François Bloch-Lainé, Paris, P.U.F., October–December 1965.

The point of departure of the fourth chapter is the article "Loisirs, travail, societé," which appeared in a special number of *Esprit* devoted to leisure, in 1959.

I owe thanks to Françoise Quarre, who re-read these texts and suggested useful corrections, and also to Yvette Duflo, Colette Didier and Fanny Penzak, who watched over the material preparation of this book.

A.T.

# Contents

# THE
# POST-INDUSTRIAL
# SOCIETY

# INTRODUCTION

❦❦❦❦❦❦❦❦❦❦❦❦

# The Programmed Society and Its Sociology

A new type of society is now being formed. These new societies can be labeled post-industrial to stress how different they are from the industrial societies that preceded them, although—in both capitalist and socialist nations—they retain some characteristics of these earlier societies. They may also be called technocratic because of the power that dominates them. Or one can call them programmed societies to define them according to the nature of their production methods and economic organization. This last term seems to me the most useful because it most accurately indicates the nature of these societies' inner workings and economic activity.

All these terms define a society according to its historic reality, its historicity, the way it acts on itself—in a word, according to its praxis. Using one term or the other represents a choice; speaking of mass societies, or societies in flux, or societies in which achievement ranks higher than heritage, represents definite choices quite different from our own. It is not a matter of opposing these choices against each other as if one or the other was ideologically preferable. We must, however, recognize that they point toward different types of problems and social facts. To define a society on the basis of its forms of social organization is to place actors in a situation and then observe their reactions to it. They will be well adapted or deviant, central or peripheral, integrated or rootless. Their actions will be defined either as opposition and resistant to change or as innovative and strategically measured. Analysis will then focus on the intentions and statements of the actors, on their interaction, exchanges, negotiations, and mutual influences—in brief, on social interplay.

The method I choose to follow is different: it will question first of all the social and cultural orientations of a society, the nature of the social conflicts and power struggles through which these orientations are worked out, and what it is that the ruling social elements repress that provokes social movements. My analysis will not focus on the inner workings of the social system but on the formation of historical activity, the manner in which men fashion their history.

## The Society in Question

It may come as a surprise that the most widespread characteristic of the programmed society is that economic decisions and struggles no longer possess either the au-

tonomy or the central importance they had in an earlier
society which was defined by the effort to accumulate and
anticipate profits from directly productive work. Such a
statement may seem paradoxical since society as a whole is
more than ever influenced by the instruments of economic growth and its tangible results. Are not all social
and political regimes measured by their capacity for development and enrichment? This does not mean that
post-industrial society, having reached a certain level of
productivity and, hence, of wealth, can abandon concern
with production and become a consumer and leisure society. Such an interpretation is belied by the most obvious
facts. The type of society we live in is more "driven" by
economic growth than any other. The individualized
features of private life, as well as local societies and their
ways of life have been profoundly affected—even destroyed—by ever-growing geographic and social mobility,
by the massive diffusion of information and propaganda,
and by broader political participation than ever before.
Precisely these factors make it impossible for exclusively
economic mechanisms to be maintained any longer at the
center of social organization and activity.

Growth results from a whole complex of social factors,
not just from the accumulation of capital. Nowadays, it
depends much more directly than ever before on knowledge, and hence on the capacity of society to call forth
creativity. All the domains of social life—education, consumption, information, etc.—are being more and more
integrated into what used to be called production factors.
This is true of scientific and technical research, professional training, the ability to program change and regulate
its elements, the management of organizations with multiple social relationships, and the communication of at-

titudes that favor the mobilization and continual transformation of all these production factors.

It is understandable that certain defensive reactions come to the surface in such a situation. They resemble certain reactions observed during the nineteenth century when industrialization overturned traditional patterns of life. Local communities, educational institutions, or particular cultures may struggle against all this upheaval and may attempt to maintain their autonomy. Their adherents sometimes hurl the accusation of "technocracy" against those who insist on the hold of economic growth and social change over every aspect of social and cultural life. But we must not forget the example of capitalist industrialization. Has the struggle against capitalism been waged more successfully by those who appealed to agrarian and craft ideals or by those who defined themselves in terms of capitalist society, organized the workers, and created the socialist idea? Our task is to recognize the new type of production, the new power, and the new social conflicts, instead of insisting on resistance by older forms of social organization and cultural activity.

It is much more accurate to view growth as conditioned by the entire political process than to conceive it as simply dependent on economic processes operating almost independently of social control. Whether the economy is conceived in terms of planning or a firm is seen as a decision-making system, strict sociological analysis demonstrates the increasing dependence of the conditions for development on the entire structure of social organization. It is apparent that, relative to the great concentrations of economic power, even the autonomy of the State is weak, indeed often illusory. The most massive investments are not governed by the traditional standard of a fair return, but are made on the basis of expansion and power.

The traditional forms of social domination have been profoundly transformed by this fact. We continue to speak of "economic exploitation" but this process is more and more difficult to isolate. The term loses its objective meaning when forced to define our consciousness of social contradictions better expressed as "alienation," that much criticized notion which is, nevertheless, more useful than ever. Social domination, now more clearly than ever before, takes three important forms.

a. *Social Integration.* The production process imposes a life-style that matches its objectives and its power system. The individual is pressured into participating—not only in terms of his work but equally in terms of consumption and education—in the systems of social organizations and power which further the aims of production. Society's bulwarks, whether built in the name of a skilled craft, lofty principle, professional independence, or a particular conception of "human nature" or cultural heritage, are reinforced by a system of production in which everyone has his place and his set roles within a regulated, hierarchical community, concerned mostly with its own cohesiveness, the condition essential to its effectiveness.

b. *Cultural Manipulation.* The conditions for growth are not limited to the realm of production; influence over needs and attitudes must also be controlled. Education is no longer in the hands of the family, or even of the school, considered as an autonomous milieu. More and more, it is transmitted through what Georges Friedmann has called "the parallel school," where the influence of those at the center of society is felt most directly.

c. *Political Aggressiveness.* This society of interlocking agencies, dominated by great politico-economic organizations, is more than ever oriented toward power and strictly political control over its internal functioning and its environment. This explains our vivid awareness of the inherent imperialism of these agencies.

It is pointless to explain these apparently diverse forms of social domination as a new stage of capitalism. They may, after all, be observed in different but very clear forms in societies that call themselves socialist. Certain small but highly original intellectual groups, such as "Socialisme ou Barbarie," * have long rejected the overly ritualistic and absolute distinction between capitalist and socialist societies with which many are too easily satisfied. This is not to say that there is no difference between capitalist and socialist societies but only that, beneath their profound opposition, there are common problems which demand a redefinition of the differences among industrialized societies.

Today, it is more useful to speak of alienation than of exploitation; the former defines a social, the latter merely an economic relationship. A man is not alienated because his "natural" needs are crushed by a "dehumanized" society, by work on an assembly line, by urban congestion, or the mass media. Such expressions only give rise to vague moral philosophy. It is easy to understand why they irritate philosophers who have learned the more exacting use Hegel made of this notion. Alienation must be defined in terms of social relationships.

A man is alienated when his only relationship to the social and cultural directions of his society is the one the

----

* An independent Trotskyite group. It published a review where some of the earliest and thoroughest analysis of bureaucracy and technocracy, especially in the collectivistic societies, appeared, under the editorship of Pierre Chaulieu.

ruling class accords him as compatible with the maintenance of its own dominance. Alienation means canceling out social conflict by creating *dependent participation*.* The activities of the alienated man make no sense unless they are seen as the counterpart to the interests of those who alienate him. Offering the workers, for example, participation in the organization of an industry without their having authority over its economic decisions leads to alienation, unless they consider such participation a strategic move in their conflict with the managers of industry. Ours is a society of alienation, not because it reduces people to misery or because it imposes police restriction, but because it seduces, manipulates, and enforces conformism.

There are new social conflicts peculiar to the society we observe being formed. Rather than simply a conflict between capital and labor, the new conflict is between the structures of economic and political decision-making and those who are reduced to dependent participation. We could use other terms and say that the conflict is between those segments of society which are central and those which are peripheral or marginal. These are the terms used to describe the opposition between the industrialized nations and the Third World. They have the advantage of reminding us that imperialist domination is not necessarily to be equated with economic exploitation but that here again it is more exact to speak of dependent participation. The burdens borne and the aid received by the underdeveloped countries are determined by the economically dominant countries. These nations may employ military intervention to maintain this relationship of dependency, even

* This term is used frequently in a technical sense and has therefore been translated literally.—*Translator's Note.*

when it is not called for to defend their strictly economic interests.

This new social conflict is inaugurated when the battle against this alienation begins and the marginal segments of society reject their assigned role, become conscious of their dependency, and begin to act with their sights focused on themselves and their self-determination. This action may even lead them to accept a lesser share of material goods in order to break out of their dependency. This conflict, however, only reaches full intensity when the will to break the relationship of dependence is joined to the effort toward independent development and, to oppose the ruling powers, appeals to the very theme of development with which the rulers identify themselves. The rejection of alienation can be simply the recognition of the social conflict between those who run things and cultural values.

This is what makes youth so important. Not that this age group is less favored than others; it is actually in a much better position than others because, in a period of rapid change, it is the least affected by obsolescence. Because youth is privileged both as producer and consumer, it is also most susceptible to dependent participation and most capable of opposition to those who identify their own class interests with economic growth. In societies which depended on directly productive labor, the skilled worker, who was relatively privileged (the difference between the wages for skilled and manual labor was greater than today), was the prime opponent of the capitalist. In a society defined by change, the group most open to change and most favored by it is the best equipped to rebel against the technocrats.

This rebellion is more social and cultural than economic, for today's social battles, like yesterday's, arouse two matching reactions among the people. They appeal to the principles generally accepted by their society and invoke them in protest against their appropriation to serve the special interests of the ruling class. Likewise, on the basis of their personal and collective experience, they resist changes which are not under the control of all the people. Young people—or any other group in society—enter the battle both because they are oriented to change and because they oppose their own experience to the counterfeit and impersonal rationality which the ruling classes use as a disguise. In capitalist industrialized societies, this resistance based on personal experience was defined by the working class and was based on one's craft or regional loyalties. Now, in the face of power which uses the weapons of integration and manipulation and is consequently able to affect every facet of social life, resistance must be mobilized in terms of the entire personality. The result is an appeal to imagination against pseudo-rationality, to sexuality against the art of compromise, to creativity as opposed to the automatic passing on of traditions and codes.

Long enervated by satisfaction with its material success, society is rejecting, not technical progress and economic growth, but its own subjection to a power which boasts of being impersonal and rational, a power which encourages the idea that it is merely the conglomerate of all the demands made by change and progress. Against this kind of social dominance, which identifies beneficial growth with itself, which considers the whole spectrum of life-styles in society merely as tools to be fitted to the needs of this growth (which it conceives as a natural rather than a social process), savage rebellion is bound to break out. The counterpart of this rebellion is always the positive struggle for creativity against the might and constraints of the power structure. Dependency becomes conflict; participation turns into confrontation.

I want to insist on one aspect of this rebellion and introduce here a reflection on the university which Raymond Aron, for instance, has already judged "preposterous." Because the protagonists of social conflict are never simply the underprivileged but also those most bound to the innovative objectives of society and therefore most subjected by it to dependent participation, the university is today becoming the privileged center of opposition to technocracy and the forces associated with it. As long as scientific knowledge did not play any essential role in economic development and could not demand consideration as a productive force, the university's role was, above all, to hand down and to defend traditional culture and the social order. The enormous numerical growth of the student population is part and parcel of the progress of scientific and technical knowledge. Education is an ever more important mark of distinction within the social hierarchy. It is becoming increasingly more difficult to think of even highly formalized knowledge as disinterested.

Politics has made its way into the university because knowledge is a production factor. But the real reason lies even deeper. The university brings together the processes of research and the rebellion of the young. As a result, it is the only major social entity that can, by its very nature, be a source of confrontation between political and economic structures. When it does not fulfill this role, it becomes—in spite of any contrary intention on the part of the teachers—an instrument of dependent participation, of alienation. Those who conceive the university's primary function as professional training are correct to be concerned about what employment the students will be prepared for at the end of their studies. Too often, however, all they actually do is train functionaries and specialists who have never been called on to critically analyze the society that will employ them. Such critical analysis may take very elemental forms such as, for example, questioning the social usefulness of the skills that have been learned. It ought, however, to be intensified to the point that it examines the social determinants of knowledge itself. For it would be naïve to believe that some kind of pure science can be constructed outside a concrete social framework and that all that need be done is to watch out that it is used for life-giving, rather than death-dealing, purposes.

Universities have entered a new phase of their existence. Their role in society has been profoundly transformed. The liberal university belongs to the past. The inescapable question now is whether the university will become the locus of integration or of confrontation. In both cases, grave dangers may threaten the creation of new knowledge, which is the specific function of the university. The student revolt could, for example, give rise to a dogmatic devotion to confrontation which would be as burdensome as conformist integration. Nothing would be more absurd than to frame the choice facing society in absolute black and white terms; but the complexity and difficulty of present problems must never be allowed to obscure the necessity of making a fundamental choice.

It would be erroneous to conclude from these introductory reflections that social struggle will quit the arena of industry and be cloistered within the universities. I will explain how—from a concrete historical viewpoint—this eventuality can be avoided. Avoided it must be, in the name of the reasoning we have so far followed.

Because the university can no longer remain uninvolved in the problems inherent in development, social conflicts which have universal significance have appeared there. If they were experienced merely as intramural problems, they would be deprived of their essential importance. The university is the privileged arena for nascent social struggles for three reasons: social constraints are less powerful there than elsewhere; the germination of ideas always precedes the organization of political struggles; the social role of knowledge is a general problem.

The programmed society will be tellingly confronted only to the degree that the struggle against dependent participation organizes itself in every domain of social life. This process will probably be gradual and difficult; it will take different forms in different countries. France—despite the exceptional importance of the May Movement—may not be the nation most rapidly involved in the process. In addition to major social organizations, urban dwellers and the consumer population must become involved in social conflict and the strugggle against dependent participation.

## Moving from One Society to Another

Under the impact of new problems and social conflicts, insufficiently organized social movements are bound to base their programs on analyses which date from an earlier situation and insist on the continuity between the great battles of the past and those of the present. It is so much more difficult to accept a break with the past than it is to come to agreement on opposition in some new situation that some continuity, in practice at least, may exist. In this way, militants in one social movement may bring their influence, commitment, and ideological formation to the movement that succeeds it. It somewhat resembles the way a new ruling class does not necessarily break with the class which ruled before it but often associates itself with it both to share a common sense of being elite and to avoid creating an opening for the forces of opposition.

Such continuity between social movements is particularly strong in France. This is partially due to the weak institutionalization of the workers' struggles and the common pattern of employer paternalism but more so to the powerful role of the State in a country where even the great capitalist enterprises are relatively weak. The power of the Gaullist State and its double role as catalyst of the fusion of two successive ruling classes and as supporter of a centralized, stratified, bureaucratic, and, in many respects, pre-industrial social organization, make it easy for the social struggles of various groups to be melded into a common attack against the political regime. The chief slogan of the general strike of May 13, 1968 is eloquent: "Ten Years Is Enough." The passage from student revolt to workers' movement, occasioned by common opposition to police repression, was guaranteed by the common struggle against Gaullism. This conjunction gave the May Movement an importance the student uprising would not otherwise have had.

We must not conclude from this historic fact that the new social movements are the prolongation or rejuvenation of the worker movement—defined according to its specific aims rather than its response to political power. (In Chapter 3, I have tried to define the present situation of the trade unions.) We are not reverting to meaningless themes like the end of the working class or the end of trade unionism. Nobody, I suppose, has seriously defended the idea that we are shortly approaching a social situation in which the workers will become a negligible category. Economic growth is still tied to the development of industry. A purely consumer society in which the industrial sector would be very much restricted and the problems of work no longer of interest to leisured wage-earners is sociological fiction. Qualified observers have correctly insisted that increased and more individualized consumption makes the demands of work more acute. Trade unionism has lost ground in certain areas but it is plausible to think that it will penetrate everywhere into tertiary, or service, activities, as it has already largely done in France. The chiefs of the industrial complex would not be so preoccupied with the problems of labor if they were not worried about new protest and socio-political militancy in a milieu they had judged conservative.

There is no reason to speak of the disappearance of the working class or of trade unionism. In any case, there is general agreement among sociologists on these simple points; those who doubt this are more anxious for polemics than for a serious examination of what has been written.

The term *working class* implies more than simply a large, underprivileged socio-occupational category. The labor movement is not the same as a tenants' association or a professional lobby. The interest attached to the problems of the working class and the labor movement is due to the fact that, in a society whose key element is capitalist enterprise, the labor movement, as the driving force of the class struggle and the demand for justice, constitutes the principal center of social conflict. The labor movement attacks ownership power; the working class is not an occupational category but a force of social struggle. The question is no longer whether workers and trade unionism may disappear, but whether the working-class movement is, today as formerly, at the center of the conflicts of society. This clear question deserves a simple answer: in the programmed society, the working class is no longer a privileged historic agent, not because the labor movement has been weakened or because it is subject to the strategy of a particular political party; still less because it has bad leaders; but simply because the exercise of power within a capitalist firm no longer places one at the center of the economic system and its social conflicts. However, in a country like France where the technocratic society is being formed out of a very traditionalist capitalist regime, the struggle against managerial power remains an essential element of the social crisis.

In the programmed society, neither firms nor unions are today the chief actors in the struggle over social power. Their roles are still important but they are situated halfway between problems of power and problems of the organization of production, on an intermediary level we shall call institutional. Their arguments and struggles are more concerned with decision-making than with power. The institutionalization of these conflicts may be gradual and incomplete but it is from now on an irreversible fact. This does not mean that our society is moving toward industrial peace; quite the contrary. It means that these conflicts do not come to grips with real social power—in the United States, the Western social democracies, or in the Soviet bloc. Countries like France and Italy, whose social organization is marked by industrial imbalance and resistance on the part of archaic social and cultural forms, are the only countries in the industrial world where the labor movement retains a certain revolutionary aura. Even there, closer examination shows that trade unionism is very far from being a revolutionary force or even a social movement actively engaged in a direct power struggle. The vehemence of the opposition, the suffocating nature of social inequalities, the frequent refusal of the State or of management to negotiate honestly, all attest the importance of vigorous worker action. But these reasons are not convincing enough to accord the working class a central role in the new social movements.

One of the significant aspects of the May Movement is that it demonstrated that sensibility to the new themes of social conflict was not most pronounced in the most highly organized sectors of the working class. The railroad workers, dockers, and miners were not the ones who most clearly grasped its most radical objectives. The most radical and creative movements appeared in the economically advanced groups, the research agencies, the technicians with skills but no authority, and, of course, in the university community.

No socio-political movement of any strength can develop unless it includes the laboring class, which contains the greatest number of dependent workers. Such opposition is too commonplace to be important and completely neglects the crucial idea that the key element in the problems, conflicts, and protagonists of historic evolution is changing. Tomorrow's struggle will not be a repetition or even a modernization of yesterday's.

## *Prehistory of a New Society*

Pressed to the utmost, this idea and some of the preceding remarks might lead one to conclude that cultural revolts are well on their way to replacing social struggles and that today's social conflicts are centered in the realm of consumption rather than production. Hasn't it been said that in May 1968 one captured words, just as two centuries ago one took the Bastille or Versailles, the symbols of the monarchy, or just as more recently one wished to take over the factories?

The new social conflicts, far from existing outside the production system, are at its very core. Indeed, they reach into new areas of social life, but only because information, education, and consumption are more closely bound than ever before to the realm of production. Under no circumstances are today's social struggles to be dissociated from economic and political power. If, very often, today's social movements attack the prevailing culture, it is less because they are avoiding economic problems than because they are only beginning. The real reason is that they are setting themselves up in over-all opposition to a social and cultural structure rather than becoming involved in a direct attack on the new ruling powers. This is due, above all, to the fact that at the present stage of the formation of the programmed society, especially in countries where the new ruling class is not yet clearly disengaged from the capitalist bourgeoisie, the social movement is up against a society that identifies itself with growth and enrichment. It is inevitable that there should correspond to the utopia of the ruling class, which identifies itself with progress, a counter-utopia which totally rejects the consumer society or the organizational constraints of production along with both old and new economic and political ruling forces. Cultural protest is only the avant-garde of social conflict. It becomes more bitter in proportion to the absence of strictly political power—the capacity to control political evolution—in the movement that supports it. There is still a wide distance between the "extra-parliamentary opposition" and the opposition forces within the institutional system. This distance may be less in Italy than elsewhere but it seems about the same in France as in Germany, Poland, Czechoslovakia, or Japan. Efforts to politically organize the protest movement have not had much success anywhere.

Some reservations are necessary about the demonstrations of the new social movements, even when they are as important as the May Movement in France. My purpose in this book is not to analyze this movement, much less to predict that it will develop progressively into a powerful political movement. On the contrary, I am tempted to believe that the history of a social movement is made up of discontinuities in its forms of action and organization. Popular uprisings, socialist utopias, and union pressures all contributed to the beginning of the workers' movement without allowing us to trace a single line of evolution which leads either to a revolutionary explosion or to institutionalization of the conflicts.

Political life cannot be simplified to a confrontation between leftists and the social system. There is no reason to believe that the first uprisings are going to give a ready-made image of a social movement which will then need only to continue in existence. Historic analysis must ceaselessly guard the sociologist against the temptation to

reduce events to a system; therefore, beyond events but
in their light, one must examine the general characteristics
of the new situation which they reveal. Their demonstrations cannot be reduced to a succession of revolutionary
days.

## The Sociology in Question

To analyze a new society accurately supposes a new approach to analysis—in the present case new in two ways:

a). Analysis of social evolution and social movements
can and must be precisely sociological. During the period
of capitalist industrialization—a process of economic transformation exceptionally deprived of social regulation, in
which capitalists act, not in a political void, but without
political regulation—analysis necessarily splits into two
branches: knowledge of the economic mechanics of capitalism and knowledge of the meaning of history. Because
society is dominated by the economy instead of the other
way around, no real sociological analysis is possible. It is
replaced by a void which separates the science of economics
from images and constructions belonging to a kind of
social thought which translates into ideas the need to
rediscover—beyond its rending divisions, beyond the accumulation of profits and the creation of the proletariat
—a social unity that is at once rational and communitarian.

Sociology did not originate directly from what one
rightly or wrongly calls the Industrial Revolution. Its
origin is contemporaneous with the establishment, at the
end of the nineteenth century, of a certain social and
political regulation of the conditions and social conse-

quences of the development of capitalism. Durkheim was its best exponent when he attempted to define the forms of a new social solidarity following the development of capitalism; but this kind of sociological analysis is limited, because it still defines society in terms foreign to the action of economic transformation. Sociology finds its proper object—and the opposition between the study of economic development and the study of the social order ceases—to the degree that economic activity becomes the result of political rather than exclusively economic mechanisms. This did not happen without difficulties nor without clashes between different schools, which were not without usefulness.

Today, while the techniques of economic analysis are formalizing the study of decisions and strategies, macroeconomics, the study of the coherence of the elements of economic evolution, is less and less separable from sociological analysis, which can no longer enclose itself in a falsely integrated world of institutions and the socialization of individuals according to the norms of the social order. The split between economic structures and social behavior has been replaced by the unifying study of historic activity, the action exercised by society on its own evolution, in terms of the appearance of cultural models, class conflicts, debates and bargaining over power, styles of organization, and the forces of change.

b) . On the other hand, this transformation of its object and its raison d'être forces sociology to renounce a too limited image of society. Even now, it too often considers society as a person, a subject taking the place of the human subject of philosophical tradition. The fundamental needs of society are only seen as a new avatar of human nature and the spirit. Some keep repeating that social behavior is made up of interactions governed within groups by norms which translate cultural values into institutions. Society appears to be built on its spirit, to be a consciousness which commands its own acts, manages its relationships to its environment, and assures its own internal order and equilibrium. Social behavior manifests both the tensions proper to every differentiated and stratified organization and the influences of values and norms. Every element of social life can be judged according to its function, that is, according to its contribution to the integration and survival of the whole. This classical sociology is today being criticized, quite properly. It has always had its opponents but they often relied overly on an ideology of progress, movement, and conflict, without bringing any positive contribution of their own to sociological analysis.

As usual, the most decisive criticisms came from a directly opposite position. The attentive study of political organizations and decision-making systems led sociology to break out of the social order. Reversing the classic viewpoint, it showed that rules and norms were often only unstable and limited agreements—the result of formal or informal negotiation—between social interests pursuing strategies which may for a time be concurrent and combinable. Today we must define ourselves according to this new sociology and not any longer according to the old functionalism. It can be called neo-liberal, because it analyzes behavior in terms of the rational quest for advantages. The multiple examples of this quest combine socially through the mechanisms of influence and negotiation and are directed not toward values but toward objectives imposed by the transformation of the environment and by competition.

This sociology plays as important a role in the new

society as classic economics played during capitalist industrialization. It corresponds to the practice and ideology of the new ruling classes. It logically affirms that adaptation to change, as well as the capacity for strategic initiatives, is more highly developed the closer one gets to the sphere of the ruling group. Those who have no initiative are more rigid and conservative, because they have "all their eggs in one basket." Certainly, one must try to increase their freedom to maneuver but it will always be limited, even though the development of new forms of work and of social organization will help. Society is most effectively governed by those who are most liberal, that is, whose strategy is most diversified. These are the rulers, the technocrats, who seek to draw the best out of any given situation and do not worry about imposing a politico-moral order which will cause rigidity, resistance to change, and the formation of a bureaucracy. They are most effective and, as a result, assure an economic progress whose principal fruit is the decentralization of decisions and tensions, which gradually brings about adaptation.

In the view of this sociology, everything takes place as if the problems of power and social conflict belonged to the past. Let us no longer speak of power, but of influence. Let us no longer speak of class conflict but of multiple tensions that are not to be suppressed but to be managed within negotiable limits. The task is not to revert to the social protests and intellectual constructions of the early nineteenth century, but to oppose to this rationalist pragmatism the existence of social movements and struggles for power. We must recall that the direction of economic growth is never assured by chess players but by particular social agents reinforcing the interests and power, no longer of a family or a private capitalist, but of a corporation.

With all the instruments of social control at their disposition, they impose dependent participation on the members of society, not only for the general objective of growth but for a particular kind of development directed by the corporations and by the exigencies of their power.

Development does not appear then to be made up of rational decisions and arbitrations. Rather, it is formed by the interplay of social struggles, dominated by the opposition between technocratic innovation and protest based on both criticism of the economic structures and the defense of personal and collective creativity, which cannot be reduced to economic effectiveness. The principal difference between the programmed society and capitalist industrialized society is that social conflict is no longer defined within a fundamental economic mechanism, and that the whole complex of social and cultural activities is involved more or less directly—but never simply—in this conflict.

Today's sociology is dominated by an intellectual confrontation between a sociology of decision and a sociology of opposition. Either of these tendencies may deny the other only at the risk of confining itself within self-righteousness and the repetition of ideology. They must struggle for an explanation of the facts. Their principal battleground is necessarily political sociology, because the term politics itself is ambiguous: it signifies simultaneously power and decision, social struggles and organizations. Since economic analysis is above all the study of economic policies, the central object of sociology is the study of politics, that is, of social negotiations out of which comes a certain institutionalization of conflicts.

For some time sociology has been tempted to reduce itself to the observation of opinions, as if social activity was only a collection of choices whose terms are entirely pre-determined. Political activity has become a form of consumption: which party or which politician will you buy? are you more or less satisfied with the policies of the government? No one will deny that it is useful to register these opinions. But doesn't one neglect the proper object of sociology—the formation of collective action through which the consumer will become the producer, a maker of his society and culture—if one stops there? Already, the study of organizations and decision-making systems has bypassed this accountability. Only the active intervention of social movements and the reappearance of major political debates can impose on sociology a return to its principal objects of study: the process of social change, the nature of power, the formation of social movements, and the creation of the future.

The essays that make up this book must be read as contributions to the study of the interplay, conflicts, and movements through which economic growth may be transformed into a type of social development, and through which there may be fostered the confrontation between dependent participation and creative opposition.

*March 1969*

# I

‧‧‧‧‧‧‧‧‧‧‧‧

# Old and New
# Social Classes

A new kind of society is being born. If we want to define
it by its technology, by its "production forces," let's call
it the programmed society. If we choose to name it from
the nature of its ruling class, we'll call it technocratic
society.

In social analysis and in practice, the notion of social
class has been too intimately bound up with the social
organization of the era of capitalist industrialization for
that notion not to be profoundly questioned in any consideration of a society in which the creation of knowledge, the systems governing production, distribution, and
information, and the network of political and economic
decisions form a social and economic organization profoundly different from the nineteenth century. Must

we abandon the idea that the class struggle holds a central place in sociological analysis? Many have been tempted to answer affirmatively simply because the analytical tools inherited from an earlier period are clearly unable to explain the new situation. Our plan moves in the opposite direction. It will affirm the fundamental importance of class situations, conflicts, and movements in the programmed society. This plan can only be realized if we detach ourselves as completely as possible from historically defined images and ideas and become involved in a radical renewal of social analysis. One could attempt to adapt the old ideas to new situations, but such an exercise would be futile because it takes no account of social practice. If we wish to retain the useful idea of social class and free it from any particular historical experience and interpretation, we must begin, not with a definition, but with critical analysis of the themes of social class and class society as they have come to us, especially in Europe. We must set out, not from a new abstraction, but from the examination of a concrete representation of social organization.

## The Historical Image of the Class Society

The nineteenth century has left us a particular historic image which many have called *class society.* The apparent clarity of this situation, however, has made it almost impossible to single out the special role played by any particular element within this social structure. We shall try first to single out the components whose combination has given rise to the over-all image of a class society.

a). There exist *social milieux* socially and culturally separated from each other. This separation is due to the slowness with which inherited social forms are changed. From generation to generation, a particular culture is passed down within collectivities in which institutional and personal relationships are inseparable. Because this situation defines individuals solely by their economic function in terms of the entire society, it is not directly connected with relations between classes, which constitute a general and abstract principle of social organization. Cultural inheritances, on the other hand, are concrete and particular. They are orderly systems that define and regulate the pattern of social relationships within a unit whose limits are set by kinship, territory, traditional occupation—situations that are ascribed rather than acquired.

From this point of view, even the traditional ruling classes are defined more by heritage than by function or by their power to dominate. The more closely a society on the way to industrialization is bound to a pre-industrial and rural society, the more important is the role of heritage. As all observers of Western societies from Tocqueville to Lipset have remarked, the resistance of traditional societies reinforces consciousness of separations and barriers, the symbols of social hierarchy. In France, we prefer to speak of the bourgeoisie rather than of entrepreneurs in order to stress the close bond between capitalists and the pre-industrial ruling classes. This bears witness to the constant desire of acquired wealth to be transformed into inherited wealth and of industrial profit to be converted into rents. The image of the idle rich man, living off the revenue of his property, playing the noble, remains very vivid in this country. So does the image of the speculator, accumulating money for himself outside of any institutionally defined social function. Nineteenth-century French literature takes cognizance of the financial speculator and the landowner; it almost completely ignores the captain of industry.

b) . *The social tensions resulting from the accumulation of wealth* have been, if not stronger, at least more weakly institutionalized in Western Europe than in parts of the world which came later to industrialization. This explains the importance in Europe of a definition of the working class as a proletariat. Mass migrations within a traditional society caused the processes of social disorganization and reorganization to be superimposed one on the other. It is characteristic that, in discussing the formation of heavy industry, one thinks first of the skilled workers and artisans, whose trades were destroyed by mass production, rather than of all the unskilled urban and rural workers for whom machine labor represented "specialization."

The beginnings of industrialization in England and France have been presented as a period of misery and social crisis. This is arguable from the point of view of economics, for, on the whole, the standard of living for the masses was not lowered. From the sociological point of view, the statement is true because the cultural uprooting and direct subjection to the pressures of competition and employer authoritarianism were not attenuated or compensated by any political regulation. The European working class was deprived of political and social rights for a very long time. Unions were able to organize only very slowly, at the cost of the lives of many militant leaders and by withstanding the most brutal forms of repression. The absence of any political regulation of industrialization caused the industrial conflict and the political conflict to be superimposed on each other, as correctly stressed by Dahrendorf.[1] Such liberal politics and the condition of the proletariat gave the worker movement its explosive force within a society essentially subject to the demands of capitalist accumulation.

In this sense, European industrialization was exceptional. Nowhere else was the economic transformation accompanied by such weak social control and by such an absence of political influence on the part of the urban and industrial workers. Most English workers waited a century —until the electoral reforms of 1884–1885—to receive the right to vote. Likewise, in Europe, there was the longest time-lag between the beginning of mass production and that of mass consumption. This extended lack of popular participation in the direction and results of economic growth is a trait of nineteenth-century Europe.

c). Industrialization was not only dominated by the heritage of the past and the pressures of the present. As it is today, it was a *projection of the future,* a societal model. The absence of a diversified social control of economic development obligated this projection to express itself in universal terms as well as within the framework of conflicting group interests. The world of business and the world of labor opposed each other but each looked to a total reorganization of society. Extensive research into the French working class [2] led us to see an opposition between class consciousness formed this way and proletarian consciousness. The latter is a sense of being excluded and exploited. The former, on the contrary, is both a defense of

[1] Ralf Dahrendorf, *Class and Class Conflict in Industrial Societies,* English edition (revised and expanded from the German work published in 1957), (Stanford University Press, 1959).

[2] Alain Touraine, *La conscience ouvrière* (Paris: Editions du Seuil, 1966).

class interests and a plan for industrial society, an appeal for rationality and progress against the irrationality and contradictions of capitalism. In the same way, one could probably distinguish between the speculator's desire for enrichment and the class consciousness of the liberal entrepreneur who—with as much good faith as the labor leaders and theoreticians—envisions a society of abundance in which misery and injustice would be eliminated.

We speak of class consciousness to stress that the conflict between models of social development is no more measured or reformist than the tension between capitalists and proletarians or than class and sectional oppositions in a traditional society. On the other hand, this type of social conflict is the best source of enduring social movements, organized and oriented according to a program of social transformation and capable of forming alliances with other occupational sectors of society. It would not be inaccurate to identify, on the workers' side, this type of social movement with socialism, taken in all its doctrinal and practical forms as a model of social organization and transformation.

The three elements just distinguished are not merely juxtaposed; they combine to form the historical image of the class society, composed of two fundamental classes with contradictory interests, engaged in an all-out contest for power and wealth, in which neither opponent can gain except at the expense of the other. Separately, none of the three elements making up the image is sufficient for this general conception of social conflict.

We have already said that the distance between cultural heritages leads to a pluralist rather than a dualist vision of society. Each group tends to define itself by its cultural and occupational particularity. Regional, religious, and occupational differences have long caused fragmentation in the peasant and laboring classes, indeed even among industrial workers. This last group is often more sensitive to the constraints arising from family and financial groupings than to those imposed by the economically dominant class.

Likewise, while a vision of social models of development may tend to prefer larger coalitions as more capable of influencing the system of political decision-making, it does not at all imply a definitive rupture between the hostile and estranged blocs. It defines individuals by reference to development; it admits on principle that their nature may be changing, that the motivating elements of each coalition may be constantly replaced by others, that the workers may be only partially able to get involved in socio-political activity.

The conflict between social models of development sets in opposition social forces and policies rather than social groups. The conception of defined classes as complete and opposed historical entities results from a combination of the "traditional" model of classes, viewed as cultural entities, and the "industrial" model of conflict among groups with different interests. It results, in other words, from a combination of a "concrete" conception of class and an "abstract" conception of class conflict, which is verified only a situation marked by liberal accumulation of wealth and maximum tension between capitalists and the proletariat. Considered in isolation, this tension could no longer explain the classic image of the class society. It leads, on the contrary, to the crumbling of all the forces present, to a crisis situation in which the capitalists fight one another through competition, while the workers, torn from their roots, subjected to insecurity and misery, can do nothing but submit, each man shifting for himself or small groups rebelling in brief outbursts of violence. What organizes the action of social classes is cultural heritage on one side and programs of action to transform society on the other. More simply, the sociological theme of social classes has no meaning or interest unless there exists a certain degree of class consciousness. Exploitation of the proletariat can define a class situation but it is incapable of explaining the formation of class consciousness and action, since every social action supposes the articulation of objectives and the definition of a social framework for collective action.

The identification of society with class conflict supposes the combination of three elements: *1*) an internal, occupational, and communal principle of self-defense; *2*) consciousness of the contradictions between the opposed economic and social interests; and *3*) reference to the general interests of industrial society. The important thing to stress is that we are talking about *an unstable combination of elements which are not sociologically contemporaneous*. It has occurred only once in the history of industrialization, during the first wave of industrial development in Western Europe. Even in this limited framework, it was never more than very partially achieved, as demonstrated by the fact that the worker movement never succeeded in unifying the working class in a revolutionary action.

## Destruction of the Image of Class Society

We must now examine the destruction of this "classical" historic image of the class society and see what happened to each of its elements when they became autonomous and independent of each other.

a) . In the mass society *living standards* replace *ways of life*. This classic affirmation may be somewhat over-simplified, but it indicates clearly the disappearance of the old cultural supports of social classes. The chief role in the process was played by urban evolution rather than by the transformation of work. Unfortunately, we know less about residential milieux than about working environments, despite the importance of studies made by the Chicago School of Sociology or by Paul Henri Chombart de Lauwe. Research in three H.L.M.'s (low-cost housing developments) in the Paris area suggests conclusions which, despite their limitations, indicate two ways in which people move beyond the older community or neighborhood spirit. Individuals on their way up the occupational and social ladder, particularly if they are workers, want a homogeneous and stratified, what we might call an "American," living situation: single family dwelling, active relationships with their neighbors, strong awareness of status differences among neighborhoods. On the other hand, with the exception of the most deprived families, individuals in a static situation show more willingness to accept a multiple dwelling which offers little opportunity to distinguish oneself socially. They also want to limit their relations with their neighbors and their social life in general. Living in close quarters with a large number of people leads to a lessening of social relationships. This second situation is especially true among relatively well-salaried employees.

In the residential situations we studied, we found almost no trace of the traditional "lower class" model which was strongly marked by social heterogeneity and broad sociability. The research of Bennett Berger [3] suggests that only in isolated and homogeneous working-class sections do people still place a high value on neighborhood social relations and possess a strong awareness of belonging to a working-class environment. The relative importance of this type of residential environment seems on the decline, given the development of the great urban complexes and the multiplication of the means of transportation. Andrieux and Lignon [4] demonstrated that the consciousness of being a worker was decreasingly alive outside the plant in consumer settings, although it remained very strong in the working situation. Even if we no longer accept the conclusions of Kare Bednarik, which interpret more than analyze the results of research, we cannot reject the numerous studies which demonstrate that young workers are much less conscious than their elders of belonging to a particular social situation, especially when they live in large cities. [5]

Much more evident still is the decay of rural life-styles and the gradual disappearance of cultural differences between city and country. At first glance, studies seem to indicate that white-collar workers are the social group which most evidences the life-styles based on class. Not that they make up a homogeneous social and cultural group, quite the contrary; but they seem, especially if one follows the analyses of Michel Crozier, [6] ambiguous, some aligning themselves with the workers or with some

[3] Bennett Berger, *Working-class Suburb* (Berkeley: University of California Press, 1960).

[4] Andrée Andrieux and Jean Lignon, *L'ouvrier d'aujourd'hui* (Paris: Rivière, 1960). New edition: Médiations, no. 44, 1966.

[5] Cf. particularly Nicole de Maupeou, Abboud, *Les blousons bleus* (Paris: Colin, 1968) and Kare Bednarik, *Der junge Arbeiter von heute* (Stuttgart: Kilpper, 1953).

[6] Michel Crozier, *The Bureaucratic Phenomenon* (Stanford University Press, 1964).

new form of lower class culture, and others identifying themselves with the middle class. These terms belong to the past and inaccurately describe the social situation of the white-collar workers who, all agree, are the most susceptible to preoccupation with social levels. This concern does not preclude the image of qualitatively different social situations, but clearly subordinates it to the related themes of stratification and mass culture, that is, to hierarchically organized participation and, step by step, to mass consumption.

It is pointless to insist at length on familiar facts. The newest idea, one that clearly indicates the importance of changes that have come about since the beginning of the century, is that "pauperism" no longer indicates a social class but rather particular groups: workers in former industrial centers now in decay, the aged, the physically or mentally handicapped, unskilled women who are heads of families, ethnic minorities, or transient foreign workers. "Poverty" covers a vast array of social problems: it no longer designates, as it did in the nineteenth century, the "labor problems." Under present conditions, defense of the working class is no longer nor can it be the same as defense of the "poor."

In the same way, the bourgeoisie is defined less and less by heritage. If the external signs of wealth are as obvious as formerly, the symbols of belonging to a higher social class are progressively less numerous and less clear. The decline of traditional social categories and life-styles is only one aspect of a more general social transformation, the formation of an industrial civilization each of whose elements is defined, no longer by its past or by its proper essence, but by its place within a system of change. Social nature has been replaced by social activity.

b) . In this sense, the idea of social class has been losing importance since the beginnings of industrialization and that of relationships between classes as an essential element of economic dynamics has been gaining. During the liberal industrialization of the West, the decomposition of traditional communities did not directly make for the formation of mutual interest groups. It led first to the formation of masses deprived of all individuality and of virtually every means of intervening in the development process. Consequently, they were defined by their privations and the exploitation that victimized them, not by the directions of their activity, which were decided for them—and outside them—by politicians who were not always revolutionary. If, at first, the dissolution of older communities was the most striking phenomenon, today the most highly visible development is that the proletariat has passed beyond this situation.

Union activity and political intervention have contributed equally to the *institutionalization of industrial conflict*. One can and must stress how limited it still is, particularly in countries like France and Italy, where the local unions inside the factories are still not legal.* Nevertheless, these restrictions cannot cancel out the capital importance of the successes that have been achieved. Without going back over the development of collective bargaining and the legal protection of wage-earners, it seems to us indispensable to insist on one important consequence of this development. It is indicated clearly by the growing importance of the concept of *organization* in sociological language. Applied first to the technical area (especially to

---

* It became so in France only following the general strike of May–June, 1968.

the job level), extended next to administration, and
then to the management of firms and even of the national
or regional economic system, it has more and more
taken on a social sense, indicating an autonomous level
of production, intermediate between technical execution and the decision-making system. An increasing
number of problems are seen to be connected with the
existence and functioning of business and industrial enterprises, especially the largest ones, considered as networks
of social and technical instruments geared to efficient
production.

The concentration of economic power has considerably
extended the autonomy of the problems proper to organizations. The reason one speaks so much of *bureaucracy* is
that the centers of decision-making are further and further
removed from the organs of execution. The engineer or
the laborer within a firm or conglomerate which com-
prises tens or even hundreds of thousands of workers, the
soldier in a modern army, the official in a national or
international administration are more and more aware of
their place in a communication network, of their capacity
to influence decisions which affect them, even, perhaps
especially, if these decisions do not affect the "political"
system of the organization. Unions or other employee
organizations set up for participation in management treat
a growing number of problems touching the setting of
qualifications, systems of remuneration, vocational guid-
ance, the distribution of social advantages, the improvement of working conditions, the regulation of hiring
practices, etc.

Each of these problems can give rise to industrial conflict and hence requires set procedures for reporting griev-

ances, for negotiation and mediation. Some have thought these procedures tended to create industrial democracy but historical practice indicates clearly that they develop without ever questioning the foundations of political and economic power in business and society. The autonomy of the organization's internal problems tends to largely separate labor conflicts from social movements with political aims. In practice, trade unionism is more and more autonomous in relation to the worker movement. It would be false to believe that the autonomy of the social problems of organizations means that "industrial peace" is being established because of the improvement in human relations and of procedures that have been established for consultation and negotiation. On the contrary, these great organizations are necessarily structured in a very hierarchical fashion at the same time as, according to the observation of Michel Crozier,[7] the members of such vast complexes define their position less and less simply by their situation and coherent interests. The lack of agreement among particular regulations and the multiplication of channels of influence are constant characteristics of great organizations. It is essential not to underestimate the importance of either of the two principal characteristics of great organizations: their hierarchical structure and their complexity. The classic literature on the organization of work has a very clear term for this situation: the *line and staff system,* at once both hierarchical and functional.

The result of this is that the employees in a firm can simultaneously have a very clear consciousness of the authority system in which they work and still have very

[7] Crozier, *op. cit.*

different visions of the firm depending on their functions. Authors, like Alfred Willener,[8] have seen in this the juxtaposition of a "functional" and a "class" vision of society. This conclusion seems excessive. Recognition of hierarchical distances, and even of the opposition between those "on top" and those "on the bottom," does not imply the true idea of class conflict. The excellent study by Popitz and his collaborators [9] in Germany showed that, although the concept of conflict with authority was very widespread among the ironworkers they studied, very few conceived society as dominated by class conflict. Just as it is possible to perceive opposition between the rich and the poor or the powerful and the weak without necessarily indicating a representation of society in terms of classes— for these oppositions may be either a consciousness of levels or the social presentation of a non-social image of the world, proceeding by opposed couples of any order whatever—so one must not mistake the recognition of hierarchies of authority for a perception of class opposition. To oppose the masters and subordinates is to recognize one's own condition as a member of an organization or a particular grouping; it is not necessarily the same as presenting an analysis of society. Benoit and Maurice [10] have shown that, in a large modern firm, the technicians were more aware than the workers of the problems connected with hierarchy and career, but they recurred less often to an analysis of the firm and its management in terms of classes.

[8] A. Willener, "L'ouvrier et l'organisation," Sociologie du travail, 1962, no. 4, pp. 332–348.
[9] H. Popitz, H. P. Bahrdt, E. A. Jures, A. Kesting, Das Gesellschaftsbild des Arbeiters (Tübingen: Mohr, 1957).
[10] O. Benoit and M. Maurice, Les relations entre direction et salariés, 2 vols. mimeographed (Paris: I.S.S.T., 1960).

This is why we cannot accept the central proposition of the important book by Dahrendorf. At first, his analysis follows a path parallel to our own. With great exactness, he describes the formation of the composite image of social classes inherited from the nineteenth century and, in particular, the Marxist conception. At the end of his analysis, he thinks he can define classes as antagonistic groups occupying opposed positions on the scale of authority in hierarchical organizations (*Herrschaftsverbände*). Wherever there are rulers and ruled, there is class conflict. This conclusion ignores the distinction, which seems to us essential, between problems of administration and problems of power; consequently it mixes situations which are profoundly different.

On one side, there exist organizations governed by centers of decision-making completely outside themselves. This is the case with public agencies governed by political power. In this case, even violent conflict between chiefs and subordinates remains within a particular organization and arises from an examination of the workings of this organization or of a particular model of authority, but not from an examination of the power system. On another side, there are voluntary organizations in which there assuredly exists an authority system within which conflicts between the base of members and the oligarchy of those in authority can develop. But these conflicts are not to be confused with class conflicts. The membership can speak of betrayal but not of exploitation or alienation.

There exists only one case in which all these situations can be mixed together and in which every conflict in an organization is the manifestation of a pervasive social conflict: totalitarian societies. Even in this case, it is quite probable that analysis is not conceived in terms of classes, but rather in terms of a ruling elite and of strictly political power.

One cannot speak of class conflict simply because the inequality of social participation has been recognized. Like skill or income, authority in an organization represents a level of participation. It is evident that the chiefs, like the rich or the skilled, may seek either to appropriate the product of the collective effort or, more generally, to direct the collectivity according to the values and interests of their own category. There is no class vision until this accusation has been made and the consciousness develops of not only a separation but of a social contradiction. Dahrendorf rightly affirms that the class problem is a problem of power but he confuses power and authority. In this way, he ends with such a general definition of classes that it includes quite different situations and runs the risk of being reduced to a very superficial conception: the opposition between those who give orders and those who take them. Are the relations between teacher and pupil, foreman and worker, soldier and officer, employee and office manager, nurse and hospital director all of the same kind? We shall answer that they are the same only to the degree that all hierarchical organizations have common problems; they are not the same if we are considering problems of power and social classes.

Frequently in a private enterprise, industrial or commerical, economic power and internal authority are both in the hands of the head of the enterprise. But is it not the merit of the sociology of organizations to have forced itself to separate the two types of problems as social practice itself more and more differentiated them? In particular, do not the managers and supervisors exercise authority without participating in power?

c) . We must again return to the theme of the concentration of power, which is the counterpart of the autonomy of the internal problems of organizations. We will not accept the image, proposed by C. Wright Mills,[11] of a power elite which acts as a defined group and cohesively defends the supposedly unified interests of all its members—politicians, economic leaders, the military. All observations belie the existence of such a unified elite, both in liberal and totalitarian regimes. Neither is it convincing to speak of a society only as the cross section of the interests of particular organizations and to affirm that the world of power no longer exists, that all that exists is authority, made twice as effective because of the influence it wields over other bearers of authority. That the road to power is becoming more and more open, that the State is not a god presiding over a world of subjects is true today, as it very likely was yesterday. The fact remains, nevertheless, that a power organization does exist. We can certainly say it is more powerful and more cohesive than formerly, that it directly commands a share of the national product which increases as the importance of its long-range economic, scientific, or military programs grows.

Should we not then reject the concept of social class and replace it with that of political class or, more simply, with the renewed opposition between the interests of the State and those of the citizenry. Unfortunately, these expressions cause more confusion than clarity. The State is not an autonomous social unit; neither is it equivalent to the politico-economic decision-making system. Like business, it can be considered an organization. On the other hand, except in totalitarian societies, the political system is not

[11] C. Wright Mills, *The Power Elite* (New York: Oxford University Press, 1959) .

the same thing as the structure of the State. It is preferable, consequently, to concentrate here on politicoeconomic power rather than on the State as institution.

Can one say that, in an advanced industrial society, this power is identified with a class? Certainly, in modern societies, the very rich and powerful are assured important advantages which can easily be denounced as scandalous. This is not, however, a satisfactory answer to the question. It is much more important to stress that advanced industrial societies are no longer societies of accumulation but of programming.

Today, the future is no longer principally guaranteed by private investments, both because the State is responsible for and directs a growing portion of economic investment and because social investments, especially in the area of education, have considerably increased. Today's largest enterprises are not mining or chemical conglomerates but space and nuclear research and the national department of education or its equivalents. The nineteenth century was aware of the opposition between exchange-value and use-value; today's principal problem is the opposition between development and consumption.

At the very moment that we recognize more clearly than ever that raising future living standards is determined by present investments, the gap between the conditions for further economic progress and the results of progress so far achieved widens considerably. Likewise, the effectiveness of investments comes to depend more and more on complex political strategy and on methods of administrative organization. Investment is no longer the function of only one sector of society, or more precisely of one class, but of the entire society. Politics no longer goes along with economic organization; it precedes and governs it. Economic progress has come to be seen as the result, the most visible sign, of the functioning of society, that is, of its ability to manage the tensions which necessarily arise from the opposition between investment and individual consumption.

d). The distinction we have just established between problems which are internal to organizations and those on the level of economic decision-making power must be understood as a distinction between different types of social problems. It would be excessive to conclude from this that the former are the concern of business and the latter of the State. One may come close to such a simple division in societies where the activities of business and industry are strictly controlled by the State but that is an extreme and very rare case. It is more important to recall the distinction between organization, as an administered system, and the firm, as a unit of economic decision-making. The conflicts proper to organizations bear on the mutual relations of their individual and collective elements. On the other hand, if a union fights for a wage increase, this is an action directed at the firm. The more liberal an industrial society is, the more important are demands and negotiations within the firm. As a general rule, conversely, in managed economies these problems are posed on a broader front. In every case, to the degree that the economic conflict within the firm ceases to be a manifestation of the class struggle, it can be interpreted in strictly economic terms, i.e., in terms of the negotiating power within the labor market of the contending parties. This also limits their alternative courses and obligates them to greater "realism." Above all, it circumscribes their negotiations within general contractual agreements or governmental regulations.

This growing autonomy of demands and wage disputes relative to the general policies of the labor movement is particularly noticeable in countries like Sweden where national agreements between the management and labor federations coexist with a wage-drift in business and industry. This autonomy is the counterpart, on the one hand, of treating the internal problems of organizations according to differing institutional plans and, on the other, of an expanded national economic policy that regulates or tries to modify wage changes as it does price fluctuations. Wage disputes are sharper to the degree that they are less integrated within general policy. Demands become more practical and shrewd to the degree that they are separated from plans for the transformation of society.

Thus, the separation of organizational conflicts from class conflicts is accompanied by a distinction between the pragmatic defense of wages and the effort to transform society. Clearly, this is an analytical distinction. Union strategy constantly combines these different kinds of problems. Nevertheless, they possess a growing autonomy. This is demonstrated by the existence of distinct channels to deal with each of them: local unions, joint consultation systems, political organizations.

## New Classes, New Conflicts

The new ruling class can no longer be those who are in charge of and profit from private investment; it can only be all those who identify themselves with collective investment and who enter into conflict with those who demand increased consumption or whose private life resists change. This formula is not complete, because it does not introduce the fundamental idea of a "perversion" of investment. Investors can identify themselves with the general interest and demonstrate very logically that their success is the condition for improvement of the general standard of living, which would be made impossible by social and political pressures for a "distributive" policy cutting the capacity for investment off. It has always been true that one can only speak of a ruling class if those who possess economic power use it, partly at least, for goals that do not foster the satisfaction of social demands; in other words, if the investment and production systems absorb for their own interests an important part of the resources that are created, or utilize them for non-economic purposes. This can happen at any level of the economic system: political decision-making, administrative organization, or technical execution.

a. On the level of political decision-making, the economic irrationality of separating investment from consumption most often takes the form of power politics, the simplest example of which is the subordination of social policy to the "imperatives" of defense, science, or economic concentration.

These problems are not only national. One of the explicit causes proclaimed during the student uprising at Berkeley was the students' dissatisfaction with a university increasingly involved in pure and applied research but uninterested in serving the students whom it considered the laboring class of science rather than human beings in the process of formation. In the same way, the medical profession has often concentrated on the problems of a patient in a way that turns him merely into one element in a system aimed at advancing the knowledge and treatment of a disease, rather than as someone who is to receive

personal "service." This is not at all intended to mean
that an increasing concern for scientific investment automatically creates social contradictions, still less that it is
socially irrational, but only that it runs the risk of creating a split between the development of techniques and
service.

*Technocrats* distend the relation between these two
terms for the benefit of a self-devouring technical development, which transforms itself into the non-rational accumulation of power and thus creates social conflicts.
Their appropriation of an excessive share of the collective
product is relatively infrequent and of no real concern,
whereas the capitalist invests only after he has deducted a
certain, sometimes very important, portion of his resources for his private consumption. While the image of
the capitalist as interested only in pure enjoyment is naïve
—and makes his role as entrepreneur incomprehensible—
it is clear that the capitalist system is often marked by
spectacular wealth and display of luxury on the part of
the holders of capital or their families. The technocrat,
on the other hand, does not live in luxury, even if his
function may gain him considerable advantages. As John
Kenneth Galbraith has remarked, the image of wealth is
today more often associated with "stars" than with the
managerial class. Even when they share in capitalist profits
—the directors of large companies whose options and
other advantages considerably augment their salaries—
they shy away from conspicuous consumption. Their
ideology is service to the State, to the party in power, to
the economy; their ethics are impersonal; their style is
manipulation rather than imperiousness.

Technocrats are not technicians but managers, whether
they belong to the administration of the State or to big

businesses which are closely bound, by reason of their very importance, to the agencies of political decision-making. Only in this sense can we speak of a "power elite," keeping in mind the conflicts which can break out among the technocrats just as they broke out among different bourgeois factions during the era of capitalist expansion. There is no need to go further and say that the technocrats completely dominate the political system. Such a statement is as excessive as presenting the nineteenth-century State as merely an instrument of capitalism, which historical studies of Marx have shown to be a great oversimplification, particularly in France and Germany.

*Technocrat* is as ambivalent a term as *capitalist*, which is used to designate both entrepreneurs and speculators. In France, for example, there exists a liberal technocracy which has played an essential role in the reorganization and development of the French economy by striving to lead French society to recognize the importance of public consumption as both a social investment and an important element of private consumption. For both general and particular reasons, one would disqualify oneself from serious analysis of our type of society, if one always gave *technocrat* a pejorative connotation. Defining class opposition does not mean separating two whole value and interest systems as if they were totally foreign to each other; nor does it mean setting up a systematic opposition between private and public interest, or government and liberty. In certain extreme cases, it is possible that a class identifies itself entirely with its own interests or with the struggle against the other class and, in the process, acquires a certain cohesiveness despite a lack of real homogeneity. Most often, each class plays several historical roles at once, simultaneously progressive and conservative, as

an element of social transformation and a force resistant
to change.

Moreover, it can happen, as is the case in France, that
the disorganization of the political system, including the
maintenance of public freedoms, gives the new rising class
a double role as economic innovators and as defenders of
consumption, especially public consumption. With only
limited power over the mechanisms of decision-making
and the presentation of grievances, they develop an ideology—well expressed in the Fourth Plan *—which preaches
the union of economic and social progress, at the risk of
running into two-fold opposition without having the
means to implement such a utopian program. They underestimate the conflict of interests in the situation.

Rejection of the simple image of a unified, authoritarian
group concerned only for power, in favor of a more com-
plicated description does not lessen the importance of
ruling class both as an analytical tool and as a concrete
social reality.

If property was the criterion of membership in the
former dominant classes, the new dominant class is defined by knowledge and a certain level of education. The
question is whether there exists a superior level of education with characteristics distinct from those of lower levels,
the acquisition of which creates a system of social selec-
tion and the possession of which acts as a symbol of membership in the higher class. The more advanced levels
within the educational systems become progressively more
specialized—but only up to a point. Beyond that point,
the tendency is reversed and education concentrates on

* The fourth 4-years plan of economic development—1962–66—under
the leadership of Pierre Massé tried to devote a larger part of public
investments to basic social equipment, in housing, education, health, etc.

the acquisition of general methods of analysis. Analogously, lower functionaries do not specialize; middle management is more and more specialized according to rank; at the top, officials enjoy great horizontal mobility. On the other hand, the education of the top level tends to be independent of any specialized body of professors and is largely provided for by members of the elite whose own education has guaranteed their success; top management officials play an important role in deciding what is taught at the Ecole Nationale d'Administration. Education tends also to be transformed into a mechanism of initiation into a particular social group and to take on a symbolic character, most often represented by attendance at a particular school or university. Entrance examinations take the place of final examinations, which indicates the relative importance of recruitment programs as opposed to the communication of knowledge.

In this way, a new aristocracy is created along with a consciousness of the separation between it and the middle echelons of the hierarchy. Between the staff and the manager, the civil administrator and the director, sometimes between even the highly placed research worker and the "boss," a separation is established and marked by many signs, including sometimes significant differences in income. A hierarchical continuity among bureaucrats and technocrats may appear to exist but it is a rare case when the members of a great organization cannot recognize the line that separates them.

Technocracy is also a meritocracy which regulates entrance into its ranks by controlling credentials. This phenomenon is perhaps more accentuated in France than in other countries, for French technocracy has been able to impose itself on the traditional State structures and the

prestige which the "great schools" * and professional
bodies have been able to preserve. The same tendency is
manifest in all industrial countries, including the United
States where many great universities are almost transformed into large professional training schools, recruiting
by competitive examination.

Once in the managerial category, one never leaves it.
Many technocrats certainly see their positions improve or
worsen, depending on whether the governmental administration is favorable to them or not. But they have great
job security and their income is safe even if they are "un-
attached." In this way, a social group is formed. It is
certainly not homogeneous but has a definite self-con-
sciousness, adopts certain behavior patterns, and exercises
considerable control over recruitment.

The technocracy is a social category because it is defined by its management of the massive economic and
political structures which direct development. It conceives society simply as the totality of the social means
needed to mobilize this development. It is a dominant
class because, in proclaiming identification with development and social progress, it identifies the interests of
society with those of the great organizations which, vast
and impersonal as they are, are nonetheless centers for
particular interests.

Technocratic ideology may be liberal or authoritarian—
these variations are of the greatest importance—but it
consistently denies social conflict, though willingly rec-

* Engineers, high civil servants, economic experts, army officers, and
a large part of scientists are trained in France not in the universities
but in schools, highly selective, and generally considered professionally
superior to the universities. The most important ones are the Ecole
Nationale d'Administration, the Ecole Polytechnique, and the Ecole
Normale Supérieure.

ognizing the existence of tensions and competing strategies. These conflicts do exist, rooted in the accumulation and concentration of decision-making power and knowledge. Technocratic organizations wrap themselves in secrecy and distrust public information and debate. They aggressively build their own power, impose more and more rigid social integration on their members, and manipulate the channels of production and consumption. They are centers of power that create new forms of inequality and privilege. On the global level, we speak of central and peripheral nations, a de facto distinction between the rulers and the subjects. Similarly, within a particular nation, there is a growing separation between the central and ruling elements within the great organizations and a new *plebs* which is subject to change beyond its control, to publicity campaigns and propaganda, and to the disorganization of its earlier social structures.

It is more difficult to define those whose interests are opposed to those of the technocrats. In a market capitalism, the wage-earners are the dominated class because they are subject in the labor market to the power of those who hold capital. In the programmed society, directed by the machinery of growth, the dominated class is no longer defined in terms of property, but by its dependence on the mechanisms of engineered change and hence on the instruments of social and cultural integration. One's trade, one's directly productive work, is not in direct opposition to capital; it is personal and collective identity in opposition to manipulation. This may seem abstract, in the sense that man is no longer involved simply in his occupational role. He is involved as worker, but also as consumer and as an inhabitant, in a word as an alien subjected to a decision-making system operated in the name of the collectivity.

This is why the role formerly played by attachment to one's trade is today played by attachment to one's *space*. The worker is not defending himself simply as a worker, but more broadly as a member of a community, attached to a way of life, to bonds of family and friends, to a culture. There was a time when the appeal to history and geography was raised by the new dominant classes, the conquering bourgeoisie, which believed in evolution and progress and was attached to the formation of great national unities and great channels of trade. Today, the dominant class relies on the economy and sometimes on the social sciences, which offer it the categories that best define its developmental and programming action. History and geography, attachment to tradition and to the soil, have become the style of thought and feeling of those who resist transplantation. Sometimes, they resist blindly, but sometimes they demand that industry move to the manpower and not always the other way around, that the entire territory be harnessed instead of only favoring the great industrial concentrations. Regional consciousness and the defense of local liberties are the principal foundation of resistance to technocracy.

The defense of the city, illustrated by Henri Lefebvre, plays an increasingly important analogous role. The urban milieu, a diversified location of social exchanges, tends to explode. Residential sections become diversified and more and more clearly stratified. The rapid growth of cities leads to the construction of dwelling units which answer the elementary need for shelter of workers but are bereft of autonomous social life. To the degree that society more rapidly modifies its environment and its own material conditions, the importance of the destruction of ecological balances and the conditions of habitability makes itself

felt more and more. At the same time as the most pathological forms of capitalism disorganize social space by
delivering it over to speculation, technocratic power,
wrapped up in its plan for growth, resistant to negotiation
and new information, destroys the capacity of society to
transform its life-forms, to imagine a new kind of space,
and to develop new forms of social relations and cultural
activities. Social struggles can no longer remain limited
to the domain of labor and business, because the hold of
economic power over social life is more general than ever
and reaches every aspect of personal life and collective
activities.

b. *Bureaucracy* is the label we give to opacity within
the economic organization. Only complex organization of
technical and human means makes progress possible in
production and productivity. Each of these organized systems has a certain inertia, because of routine and from the
need to stabilize the relations among the various parts of
the whole. Each system realizes that the more complex
an organization is, the more necessity there is to devote
an important part of its resources to the treatment of
its internal problems. In the same way, a complex machine
can function only part of the time and resetting, repairs,
and maintenance create a wide gap between theoretical
and real production. This does not, however, keep a
modern machine from having a greater return than an
older one.

Internal functional demands may be transformed into
an autonomous system with its own rules and relationships. For example, if there must be a hierarchy of functions, professional activity can still be disrupted by an
overriding concern for career-building, pointless multiplication of the signs of social rank, or technically un-

justified expansion of the hierarchical ladder. Like the government service, the university and the health services, the industrial world knows the problem of W. H. Whyte, Jr.'s "organization man," [12] a mixture of conformism and opportunism, sometimes mixed with a concern for good "human relations" which gets in the way of difficult decisions.

Dahrendorf, following Renner, defined bureaucrats as a "service class" (*Dienstklasse*). But this definition is not well adapted to the new situation we have to describe. It fits better an older system of organization, the State structure (the Prussian *Beamtentum*), and the civil-service officials whom the French fear and mock.

This rigidly hierarchical, military type of bureaucracy, in which each person is defined by the delegation of authority he has received, belongs essentially to the past even when it manages to survive. Each administrative reform strikes a blow against it and it seems particularly ineffective when production tasks are assigned to it, as is the case with many public services. The inertia of a modern bureaucracy does not result from its rigidity but from its complexity and the interrelations woven among services, bureaus, and functions. While definite orders are deformed to an absurd degree as they descend through the hierarchy, there are endless conferences designed to insure respect for the interests of the participants and the slowing down of the whole organization.

Resistance comes, not any longer from the inertia of the base which lacks initiative, but from the defense mechanisms of the big and little wheels in all the parts of the organization chart; it comes from the formation of

[12] William H. Whyte, Jr., *The Organization Man* (New York: Simon & Schuster, 1956).

classes, alliances, coalitions, and schools of thought which throw the system into confusion. They transform the system into a patchwork of baronies and fenced-in hunting preserves. This is how it is with bureaucrats: adept at change, agents of progress beyond doubt, but also often careerists, vain, distrustful, absorbed in their subtle strategems and their desire to reinforce their own importance by holding back information, by fostering their own prestige in every way possible, and by defending the internal demands of the organization in opposition to its external purposes.

We must retain one important idea from Dahrendorf's analysis. The bureaucrats do not make up the whole of the "new middle class," nor even the whole of the intermediary levels of a great organization. Beside them there exist increasingly important masses of *employees* and *technicians* whose power, in terms of negotiation, authority, and influence, is weak or non-existent. We are not thinking of the new "proletariat," the employees whose tasks are as repetitive, monotonous, and restrictive as those of assembly-line workers. Rather, we are thinking of relatively advanced groups: technical workers, designers, higher ranking office workers, and technical assistants who do not take part in the bureaucratic game and who are more directly exposed to its consequences than the traditional workers, who are relatively protected by the weakness of their involvement and their great numbers at the base of the organization charts. These technician-employees represent the principal focus of resistance to the bureaucracy, while the immense mass of "clients" of the administrations represent a quasi-group which gives its protests concrete expression only with great difficulty.

This analysis seems to us to explain better the observable extension in France of the collective presentation of grievances by these middle-level professional categories than overly general ideas about their revolutionary capacities. The technicians are not taking over the place of the skilled workers at the head of the class struggle. Certainly, as a new social category begins to become conscious of its situation, it is easy to resurrect doctrines or an extremist vocabulary which directly question the principles of social organization. The collective energy of the technicians is much more directed toward redress within their organizations and protest against the bureaucracy, as well as the defense of employment status and careers. The forms of these efforts are often new and their strength is felt to the degree that economic circumstances and the short supply of technicians on the market give this group considerable power at the bargaining table—but the inspiration is not revolutionary.

c. On the level of *technical execution,* the most striking fact is the rapidity of change. Engineers, research centers, and laboratories are intent on accelerating the "obsolescence" of the techniques in use. The life expectancy of machines, procedures, and formulations is continually being shortened. It is difficult to measure how much waste is created in this way. Many observers, however, have noted that important expenditures for equipment (calculators, for example) are made without careful study of operating costs, simply because a new machine is a symbol of modernity. The gadget craze is not restricted to individuals; it is equally widespread in business and administration.

*Technicists* form a category with little chance of transforming itself into a social class, for two reasons: they are dispersed and, above all, they succeed at their excesses only if they are also technocrats or bureaucrats. We do not, as a result, include them in a list of the new social classes.

Technicism reveals itself best by its incapacity to grasp the whole picture of the problems an organization poses. The complexity of a social system is broken down by recourse to rules which are often nothing but rituals. For a long time, the critics of the so-called scientific organization of work have demonstrated the errors resulting from the reduction of human work to a succession of elementary movements and of the worker psychology to an impoverished image of *homo oeconomicus.* Both factories and administrations are aware of the rigidity of this technicism against which the skilled workers rebel especially.

One category of victims possesses a particular importance. The obsolescence of techniques is accompanied by the obsolescence of skills. A more and more numerous category of obsolete workers is formed, men forty or forty-five years old—sometimes even, in areas where techniques evolve quickly, thirty or thirty-five years old— newly created half-pay workers, the second part of whose active life is a long decline cut up by unexpected unemployment or sudden ruin. The "old"—these obsolete workers as much as the retired—are more and more precisely a new proletariat, as rejected and exploited by progress as others were by property.

The young can find themselves in a similar situation to the degree that their training either does not correspond to the needs of the economy or is underemployed when the labor market is unfavorable to them. What we too easily call the lack of adaptation of certain groups of workers is rather the sign of a social system in which training and employment are not organized so that technical and economic evolution produces the maximum professional and personal advantage for all and in which individuals are not protected by sufficient powers of social intervention.

d. These conflicts are all of the same nature. They predicate opposition between managers driven by the desire to increase production and adapt themselves to the imperatives of power and individuals who act less as workers defending their wages than as persons and groups seeking to maintain their sense of personal life. What these wage-earner/consumers seek is *security*, that is, a predictable and organizable future which will allow them to make plans and to count on the fruits of efforts they have willingly made.

The principal opposition between these two great classes or groups of classes does not result from the fact that one possesses wealth or property and the other does not. It comes about because the dominant classes dispose of knowledge and control *information*. Work comes to be less and less defined as a personal contribution and more as a role within a system of communications and social relations. The one who controls exerts influence on the systems of social relations in the name of their needs; the one who is controlled constantly affirms his existence, not as member of an organization, element of the production process, or subject of a State, but as an autonomous unit whose personality does not coincide with any of his roles. This is the reason—in our eyes justified—why the idea of *alienation* is so widespread. We are leaving a society of exploitation and entering a society of alienation.

What dominates our type of society is not the internal contradictions of the various social systems but the contradictions between the needs of these social systems and the needs of individuals. This can be interpreted in moral terms, which has aroused scant sociological interest because there is nothing more confused than the defense of individualism against the social machinery; it is easy to move beyond this kind of interpretation. As Galbraith has vigorously reminded us,[13] economic progress depends more and more not only on the quantity of available labor and capital but on the ability to innovate, to accept change, and to utilize every work capability.

A mechanical conception of society runs up against the resistance of individuals and groups who, out of hostility to being manipulated, limit their production and adopt a passive attitude toward organizations and decisions in which they do not participate. This was the case with Taylorism.* In a society which is progressively more tertiary—one in which the treatment of information plays the same central role that the treatment of natural resources played at the beginning of industrialization—the most serious form of waste is the lack of participation in decision-making. It is symptomatic that all studies demonstrate that the first condition of such participation is information. This observation, however, has more profound consequences than many are willing to face. Being informed means more than merely knowing what is taking place. It means being familiar with the background, reasons, and methods which lead to a decision and not merely with the reasons alleged to justify it. This is why unions or consultation committees ask to see the balance sheet of a firm, and to know the sources of the various categories of

[13] John Kenneth Galbraith, *The Affluent Society* (New York: Houghton Mifflin, 1958) .

* Fréderic Winslow Taylor and his followers relied mostly on individual wage incentives to foster workers' willingness to increase production.

The Bedaux system was between the wars one of the most widespread systems of job study. Every job was characterized by a certain proportion of activity and rest. The criteria on which such a proportion was established were secret and were never supported by scientific studies.

its revenue. Information is necessary to make decisions.

The central importance of this problem is underlined by the difficulties involved in any attempt to solve it. This is not simply because those who possess the information resist sharing it and prefer to retreat behind pseudo-sociological statements. The difficulties are also due to the fact that access to information presupposes a new attitude toward claims and grievances, acceptance of economic rationality, rejection of the idea that society is entirely dominated by conflict among private interests, recourse to experts whose relations with those responsible for action are difficult, etc. Seeking information is an expression of an active social politics. Lack of information (hence of participation in the systems of decision and organization) defines alienation. The alienated individual or group is not only the one left on the sidelines, subject to control or deprived of influence; it also includes the one who loses his personal identity and is defined only by his role in the system of exchanges and organization. It includes the consumer pushed by advertising and credit to sacrifice his economic security for the sake of goods whose distribution is justified by the interests of the producer rather than by the satisfaction of real needs. It includes as well the worker who is subject to systems of organization whose over-all efficiency does not balance their exorbitant human cost. As class conflict over property loses its importance and explosiveness by being localized and institutionalized, the new conflicts focus on the direction of society as a whole and arouse defense of self-determination.

e. We have just defined the principal social conflicts of programmed societies. The experience of societies characterized by capitalist industrialization is that those groups most subject to social domination are not necessarily the ones who most actively lead the fight. The further removed they are from the centers of power, the more exploited they are and the more their struggle is limited to the defense of the material conditions of existence, and it is difficult to move them to the offensive. Such responsibility must be borne not only by groups whose capacity to resist is greater—intellectuals or skilled workers with a higher standard of living and education or a stronger position in the labor market—but also by those who participate more directly in the central mechanics of economic progress.

The struggle is not led by marginal social elements who can only rise up for brief periods or support offensive action with their mass, but by central social elements who, in their opposition to those who hold power, use the instruments of production which their opponents claim to control. This used to be the role of the skilled workers; today, it is the role of those who possess scientific and technical competence. They are closely connected with the great organizations but their identity is not defined by their hierarchical authority in them. Often they even enjoy great independence from the organizations that utilize their services. They are agents of development, for their work is defined by the creation, diffusion, or application of rational knowledge; they are not technocrats, because their function is defined as *service,* not as production.

On the highest level, that of the technocrats, such individuals are the *professionals,* the members of "professions," two of which are of particular importance in our societies: teaching and public health. Professors, researchers, and physicians, who are neither salaried managers nor for the most part members of liberal professions, are in a mixed situation. Their activity requires the existence of rationalized organizations, schools, universities, research laboratories, etc.; however, its aim is to maintain or reinforce the production capacity of people rather than material production as such.

Students and patients are the direct consumers of teaching and medicine. Of course, there exist intermediary zones in which professions and production structures are mixed, particularly in research organizations, but that is not enough to wipe out the difference in kind between managerial categories and professionals. Professionals are defined much less by their hierarchical authority than by their scientific competence. One cannot speak here of social class, for the professionals are not one of the elements of a social conflict; they form a category which sometimes joins the technocrats and sometimes fights them. This two-sided situation can confer on them a higher prestige than any other category but can also lead them to a doubly irrational corporatism which irritates both technocrats and consumers.

On a lower level, where we have placed the bureaucrats, we meet the *experts*. They take part in the functioning of organizations without entirely belonging to them, even when they are on the payroll: consulting engineers, accountants, jurists, psychologists, labor physicians, instructors, and educators. Their number is increasing rapidly and will grow even more in the coming years. They constantly remind the organizations in which they are involved of their external functions. At the same time, they can bother the efficient functioning of these organizations by opposing their general principles to the empirical complexity of a technical and social communication network. Like the professionals, they may be merely external agents of firms and organizations; more often, they are able to force them to liberate themselves from their internal problems and to adapt better to society as a whole. This is one way of reinforcing the bond between investment and consumption.

Among those who carry out technical tasks, the formation of militant elites and centers of opposition is more difficult. This is true even though this category of personnel directly experiences the power of their managers and organizers, in every aspect of their lives. Nevertheless, skilled workers, progressively more subjected to the constraints imposed by business and industry, and particularly the young workers whose training is badly used by their employers, continue to play an important role. Whereas these groups used to be at the center of the social struggle, they are now only one element within it, just as a factory manager now plays only a subordinate role within the network of economic and political managers.

The general principle of our analysis is that the formation of social classes and class action has a better chance in the social and economic groups where the contradiction between organizational interests and personal autonomy—the opacity created by technocracy—is most directly manifested, i.e., at the heart of the great production and economic decision-making organizations. To be more precise, the groups which demonstrate particularly sharp resistance to the domination of technocrats, bureaucrats, and technicists are those who are associated with the life of great organizations, feel themselves responsible for a service, and whose activity puts them in constant touch with consumers. Interest groups on one level and, on another, engineers and research technicians may succumb to the contradiction born of their double identity as profes-

sionals or experts and as men of the organization or po-
tential technocrats. Sometimes, they overcome it through
militancy. Sharing the values of rationality and technical
competence which impress themselves on industrial societies, they defend at the same time the autonomy of their
working conditions and careers and set the internal
exigencies of their professional group against the pressures
exerted by the system of organization and decision-making.

In the nineteenth century, massive movements dedicated to social change were formed by the combination of
the craftmen's resistance with the realization of exploitation on the part of certain categories of unskilled workers.
Likewise, one can predict that, today and tomorrow, these
opposition elites must form the avant-garde of new movements for social change by mobilizing those communities
which are in a state of decline: aged workers who are victims of change and the "users" of hospitals, housing projects, and mass transportation.

For such an alliance to work, sufficient means must be
available to mobilize opinion. The very importance of
these means, however, generally places them under the
control of businessmen and those in power. We cannot
describe here the stages by which such mobilization may
take place, but we must, if only to put some order into a
badly organized vocabulary, distinguish different types of
"social forces." *Social classes* are on the same level as the
power system. *Special-interest groups* exist on the level of
organizations or particular collectivities. *Pressure groups,*
situated on the level of the technical organization of production or consumption, have even less direct relation to
political action. If one accepts this distinction, then we can
say that the "working class" is progressively being replaced
by a federation of special-interest groups, while groups

organized for defense of local or regional interests—traditional examples of pressure groups—can become a kind of class.

A social class or a class movement always strives to interpret in its own terms or bring under its influence the special-interest and pressure groups which are related to it. Social politics becomes more complex because the associations which are instruments of a class, a special-interest group, or a pressure group, frequently remain attached to a particular conception of their role, even while they may actually be performing others. At the same time, they can reverse the process and become spokesmen for new social forces.

These distinctions explain the special role of students in the formation of new class movements. Because they are uncomfortable with the forms of special-interest or pressure groups and are not bound by the constraints of great production organizations, they commit themselves more directly than do others to a class action against economic power. The importance of knowledge in the developmental process gives them a role which is no longer only that of avant-garde, often held by the intelligentsia. At least some of them are directly and personally involved in the new relationships of control and domination. Our analysis has concentrated on economic life as a whole because students and other university people never act in a way that reveals new social conflicts unless they move beyond the problems rooted in the crisis and transformation of the university. Students are neither simply an avant-garde nor the entirety of a new class movement. In the university, this movement and the conflicts that form it are revealed and expressed most easily. Student action—

which we shall examine in detail in the next chapter—
cannot be analyzed simply as the expression of a new
social movement. In other words, we cannot discover the
meaning of student action unless we see it in the framework of the social problems of the programmed society.

The student situation should recall that social movements are not sparked only by militant elites. The labor
movement found its real power only when working-class
elites joined their action with large masses of unskilled
workers to control the conditions of employment. In the
programmed society, likewise, new social movements can
be formed only by an encounter of the militant elites we
have just named with the groups which experience most
directly and are most vulnerable to the effects of managed
social change and which, as a result, feel their collective
identity most threatened.

## The New Industrial Societies

a) . The foregoing analyses are summed up in the chart
on the following page.

We would not attach such great importance to the class
structure of a society, if the different levels of domination
and social conflict did not overlap to a large degree. This
remark recognizes the great importance of the concept of
*techno-bureaucracy* proposed by Georges Gurvitch [14] which
indicates the connection of technocracy with bureaucracy
and with technicism. The existence of great production organizations—simultaneously oriented more toward power
than progress, bureaucratized rather than organized, and

[14] Georges Gurvitch (Editor), *Industrialisation et technocratie,* 1949,
pp. 179–199.

| DOMINANT CLASSES | DOMINATED CLASSES | EXTREME CASES OF ALIENATION | INDEPENDENTS | CENTERS OF RESISTANCE TO THE DOMINANT CLASSES |
|---|---|---|---|---|
| Technocrats | Those who are managed | Members of communities in a state of decline | Professionals | Salaried professionals and students |
| Bureaucrats | Employees | "Manual" technicians | Experts | Research technicians |
| Rationalizers | Operators | Aged workers | Service workers | Maintenance workers |

technicist rather than rationalized—constitutes one of the most important social problems of advanced industrial societies.

This problem grows in seriousness and its consequences become graver as the unity of the political, economic, and military decision-making system grows. The extreme form of this social pathology is *totalitarianism,* the subjection of the whole society to the instruments of economic development and social progress, sacrificing its proper goals for the sake of power. Totalitarianism is distinct from despotism, which is the absolute power of the State. Despotism is generally harsher to the degree that the area of the State's action is more limited and the State presents itself less as the instrument of development and progress and appeals to other principles of legitimacy: national defense, the safeguarding of the interests of a supposedly naturally superior group, or heredity. A totalitarian regime reveals itself less by monopolizing wealth than by the *absolute control of information* in all its forms, from the content of the mass media to school curricula and the doctrines of youth movements.

b) . In face of these threats, embodied in political domination rather than in private profit, it would be illusory to appeal to the "working class" for resistance, unless we give the term a very vague meaning, designating all who take orders and are subject to rules, along with everybody who lives on a salary and listens to or watches the programs broadcast for them. Such a new use of an old idea entails more disadvantages than advantages. In particular, it encourages the erroneous belief that opposition to new forms of social domination must come from the same social groups as it did formerly, which seems belied by the facts.

Likewise, it is anachronistic to attempt to depict social armies confronting each other. As we pass from societies of accumulation to programmed societies, relationships of power become increasingly more important than opposition between social groups. The result is that social movements cannot be "primary," that is, rely essentially on internal initiatives for the satisfaction of grievances and on the role of "militants" who rise up from the ranks. This process of internal formation retains undeniable but limited importance. The gap between the direct expression of a social problem and its transformation into a social movement continues to widen, which enhances the role of mass information and the formation of opposition elites.

c). The condition of the proletariat in a society on its way to wealth and the institutionalization of labor conflicts can no longer be the central theme of social debate. On the contrary, the regulation of information, local autonomy, the freedom and independence from the state of the universities, the adaptation of work to manpower, and fiscal policy are the objects around which social movements can, and do, organize.

One can even advance the hypothesis that the most "perceptible" social problems are those in which the technocracy, consumers, and professionals find themselves most directly in confrontation, that is, those problems posed by education, public health, and the organization of social space. Public opinion takes account of them less easily than labor problems, which have long ago been explained by the unions. It does not seem to be less aware of them, however, since today they possess a universality not found in labor problems, which are fragmented by the diversity of collective bargaining. In addition, they have direct political importance, since they focus not on economic mechanisms but on the systems of social decision-making. We cannot develop these propositions here, but it was indispensable to present them at least briefly, because the sociology of social classes is distinct from the study of social stratification only to the degree that it defines the domains, objectives, and instruments of the power one part of society exercises over the other parts.

The study of capitalism gave importance to the analysis of social classes in societies of private accumulation; the violence of class conflicts added drama to such analysis. Today, study of the control of economic and social equipment allows us to define present-day social forces and helps us to foresee the formation of new social movements in societies defined both by economic programming and the increasing demands of private consumption. From this perspective, one can appreciate the full importance of the study of changes and reactions to change. It is risky to speak of resistance to change, because this expression may tempt us to think of change as necessary progress which only ignorance, habit, or traditionalism could oppose. On the contrary, the most important task is to sort out under what conditions change becomes progress, how workers or, more broadly, social agents can participate in social transformations and control them, how they can defend themselves against arbitrariness and how to replace the pretended demands of rationality (like Taylor's "one best way") * with open debate on the ends and means of development. The principal objective of modern social movements is more the control of change than the struggle against profit. We must guard against two contrary errors:

* According to Taylor there is "one best way," scientifically determined, to realize a given technical operation.

*1*) believing that over-all social conflicts have been replaced by a great number of particular tensions or conflicts; *2*) being satisfied with an *aggiornamento* of the analyses which applied to liberal capitalism.

We avoid these opposed errors only by stressing the decline of "real" classes, concrete groups defined by a particular kind of social relations and culture, and the formation of new classes more directly defined by their relationship to change and the power to manage change. The dominated classes are no longer defined by wretchedness but by consumption and the tasks they carry out, hence by dependence on the forms of organization and culture worked out by the ruling groups. They are no longer excluded; they are integrated and used.

In modern societies, a class movement manifests itself by direct political struggle and by the rejection of alienation: by revolt against a system of integration and manipulation. What is essential is the greater emphasis on political and cultural, rather than economic, action. This is the great difference from the labor movement, formed in opposition to liberal capitalism. Such movements are scarcely beginning but they always talk about power rather than about salaries, employment, or property.

In earlier societies, mass movements always appealed to community and to labor against the rulers who enjoyed personal privileges without being producers. In the programmed society, the rulers are the organizers of production and are less interested in defending personal privileges than the power of the structure. Action against them is not focused on the defense of a real group; it is both revolt against a multiform control and a struggle against power.

In capitalist society, socialism was the will to conquer

the State in order to bring down the power of the capitalists. But the separation of the State and civil society belongs to the past, since executive power has been replaced
by what Bertrand de Jouvenel calls "active power." Mass
movements are less turned toward properly institutional
action and call rather for self-management, that is, for revolt against power. They will be able to achieve lasting importance only if this libertarian militancy binds itself
intimately to a program to transform economic policy.
This bond will demand a long and difficult effort.

This is the source of problems for sociological analysis.
If it records directly observable behavior and opinions, it
risks being blind to new tendencies. Only careful study
of nascent social movements, their internal contradictions
and their effective action rather than their ideologies, can
isolate the new nature of social conflicts and movements in
our society.

d). It would be a very bad defense of the importance of
class conflicts in programmed societies to reduce all social
problems and collective conduct to this one phenomenon.
Too often, two quite independent propositions are confused with each other: the first affirms the central role of
class conflict in social and political dynamics; the second
contends that, in the last analysis, the essential elements
of social behavior must be analyzed in terms of classes and
class conflicts. This second proposition has given the notion of class its political importance. But it arbitrarily
impoverishes sociological analysis and even, under present
conditions, when new classes and new class conflicts are
being formed, ends paradoxically by weakening the analysis of class relationships, because it detects them everywhere in general and nowhere in particular.

One cannot maintain the validity of an analysis of society as a class system, as we wish to do, unless one also affirms that class problems constitute only one kind of social fact. Indeed, it is all the more important to reflect on them since general opinion tends not to pay them sufficient attention. Their manifestations and consequences, it must be admitted, are not always more spectacular than those of other problems connected with social stratification or with the threat of atomic war. There are problems not connected with the system of social classes but with society in general or with particular organizations. There are those that Ralf Dahrendorf discusses and that Talcott Parsons, although sometimes wrongly accused of being only interested in consensus and social equilibrium, describes with great clarity.[15] Inequality of skill, education, and authority not only causes tensions and conflicts but tends to establish social groups which form a particular culture and give their children different basic opportunities.

The image of large organizations given by Michel Crozier can be extended to the whole of society and can encompass the conclusions of Jean Meynaud and the observers of pressure groups. We are witnessing a dislocation of the social hierarchy caused both by the multiplication of middle-level categories and by the increasing complexity of the channels of influence. This causes a greater collective insecurity, a frequently anarchical development of competition and bargaining among social groups, organizations and professions, greater and greater difficulty in adapting to rapid change, and the development of the social and ethnic prejudices stressed by Ja-

[15] Particularly in his *Essays in Sociological Theory,* new edition (Glencoe, Ill.: Free Press, 1954) , pp. 328–33.

nowitz [16] as a consequence of strong social mobility.

The important fact is that problems originating from differentiation, mobility, and social change appear less and less as signs of a more general class conflict. They are different in kind. Stratification and social class are not just two notions distinguished for the sake of analysis. They are, first of all, two distinct complex realities. Their real difference is one of the basic reasons for the dissociation of class problems and political problems—not that class problems do not have political expression. On the contrary, such expression, as we have said, is more direct than ever because class opposition is now more directly defined in terms of the control of socio-economic decision-making power. The political system is both a system of influence and an instrument for making decisions which affect and reflect class structures. Political parties are both coalitions striving for an electoral majority and programs of collective political action which can be analyzed in terms of classes. Our analysis, then, stands midway between that of Dahrendorf, for whom classes are the expression of the unequal distribution of authority within organizations, and the view that sees—either approvingly or not—the inauguration of a techno-bureaucratic regime as either inescapable or at the very least threatening.

Class structure is defined in terms of social and economic power, not in terms of organization or a political regime. This allows us first to say that class structure can be studied in all types of industrial societies and to oppose the idea that a single general type of industrial society, defined by the domination of techno-bureaucratic power,

[16] Morris Janowitz, "Some Consequences of Social Mobility," *Acts of the Third Sociological Congress* (London, 1956), vol. III, pp. 191–201.

is in process of formation. Just as a capitalist society can be defined by the type of forces and groups which have access to political power—former ruling classes, urban masses, the military, local politicians, etc.—there is no reason to believe that a society in which the techno-bureaucratic threat exists is completely analyzable from this single point of view. The conditions under which the accumulation of capital took place—whether in the name of national capitalists, a foreign power, or nationalist or revolutionary political leaders—continue to profoundly influence all advanced industrial societies; non-ruling groups do have access to power—to varying degrees, but rarely not at all.

Even more importantly, the existence of technocratic power does not automatically exclude the existence of a political process, including the political expression of more or less diversified and articulated social demands. It only works differently when the governing powers renounce their role in development solely in order to defend an institutional structure. In this case, they cease to act as a social class in order to act as a governing political group. Technocrats do not simply defend their own power. The objectives of development have autonomy relative to the social management of growth and change. This leaves room for social pressure to exert itself in the name of development and in competition with management. Class conflicts exist only to the degree that there is a political process. If this process is narrowed simply to the power of the governing group, class conflicts are replaced by purely political struggle. The work of economic development and the desire for social transformation assume very different relations depending on the varying conditions of economic and social change.

The more major obstacles a society must overcome in order to industrialize, the more firmly bound together "at the top" of that society are the demands for development and for democracy. The extreme case is a revolutionary government that seeks to insure both growth and new forms of social participation, most often at the price of strong political, or even dictatorial, controls. In this case, power is both very technocratic and very "popular," as demonstrated by the subjection of all elements of the social organization to the powerful control of one party and its ideology. That such a system can lead to totalitarianism we have already noted, but such a regime cannot be called technocratic: party spirit and ideological loyalty are stronger principles than the service of technical and ideological rationality. This theme appears constantly in the declarations of present-day Chinese communism.

To the degree that a society has been able to modernize without grave internal crises and without having to overcome resistance on the part of former ruling classes or foreign domination, the cohesiveness of the governing elites will be weak and democracy may be achieved by liberal methods. The result is that the citizens are more subject to economic pressures and controls than to political obligations.

These two extreme types of societies function in almost entirely different ways. There is no reason to think that these differences will disappear, especially if we consider the growing economic distance between developed and underdeveloped nations. As a result, it is arbitrary to define a regime simply by the greater or lesser power held by technocratic managers. The dominated classes are not merely the victims of their rulers; these, in turn, are not purely the expression of the self-interest of the production apparatus. Class conflict does not define the internal mechanism but the debate between a determination to achieve development and a demand for social democracy. These two considerations cannot be equally defended by the same individuals. Nor can they be set in complete opposition by separating managers purely interested in production from those who are managed, seen as single-mindedly concerned with consumption and direct partici-pation. It can happen that these two principal normative orientations of an industrial society are mixed in differing degrees in all social groups, or that the dichotomy within the society may be very accentuated. But there is no in-evitability that favors this latter condition. Nor is there any general type of industrial society, from the most liberal to the most authoritarian, that is by its nature most favorable to the formation of a technocratic regime.

This study has concentrated on the evolution of social facts rather than on the definition of a concept; it is now necessary to draw a general conclusion about the useful-ness of the nation of social class for the understanding of advanced industrial societies. This conclusion can only pick up a proposition that has already been presented. Along with the transformation of industrial society, we have witnessed the disappearance of classes as social "be-ings," [17] as real social and cultural milieux, and the cor-responding increased importance of class relationships as an appropriate analytical principle for social conflicts.

So long as progress is achieved by the accumulation of wealth by a particular part of society (the State treasure, the great landowners, capitalist enterprise), society re-mains divided between the great mass of those who live in

[17] Raymond Aron, "La classe comme representation et comme volonté," *Cahiers internationaux de sociologie,* XXXVIII, 1965, pp. 11–29.

a subsistence economy, with the only resources available to them those necessary to sustain the manpower supply, and the tiny group of those who monopolize the surplus flowing from conquest, commerce, or profit. Society is dominated by this internal contradiction.

Almost from its beginnings, industrialization radically transforms this situation. The rapid increase in available resources emphasizes investment in place of accumulation. It then transforms investment into productive equipment, a broader notion which includes all forms of rational preparation and use, not only of what one calls production factors, but increasingly of the organizing and decision-making systems which set these factors in operation. Schumpeter, one of the first to insist on the role of the entrepreneur, defined a change whose importance has been broadened by later studies of economic organization and planning.

Productivity, efficiency, the rationality of educational policies, land management, the organization of communications and authority systems in large organizations—it is more useful to analyze these elements of economic progress than the traditional "production factors," capital, labor, and land. No longer is it the concentration of available surpluses but the rational organization of human and technical equipment that governs economic development. Under these conditions, the idea of two basic classes that constitute separate milieux, one reduced to subsistence, the other to managing surpluses, loses its importance. With this in mind, we can affirm the incompatibility in principle between the existence of social classes, conceived as social beings, and industrial society; just as the maintenance of "inherited" situations is incompatible with the formation of a society based on acquisition and achievement. Does this mean that advanced industrial societies no longer have class structures but only a system of social stratification along with an increasingly complex political system within which pressure groups and coalitions, formed to conquer the centers of decision-making, compete with each other? We do not accept this conclusion, as we indicated in our discussion of the formation of new social classes.

Economic growth and social change are governed by a more or less unified network of decision-making and organizational structures. In opposition to these structures, resistance or revolt appear, as well as a desire for the democratic control of the instruments and results of growth and change. "Real" classes are formed to the degree that social domination is no longer concentrated and that the dominated groups are conscious enough of their own interests to defend a counter-model of development instead of simply opposing social interests to economic pressures. The nature of the groups formed in this way defines different types of programmed societies but, no matter how different they may be, their social conflicts uniformly focus on the directions to be taken by development.

To speak of social classes is to point to class problems rather than to define groups. It is simply the terminus of an evolution that began with the beginnings of industrialization. While it has maintained the machinery of capitalist accumulation, it has also forced us to consider a system of social activity rather than of social beings. The analysis of social classes no longer offers a general framework for the understanding of industrial societies; it is only one element in this understanding. This may dilute its dramatic appeal but it does not lessen its importance. Along with the study of the social system, its stratification and the relations among its elements, along with a political analysis of the conflicts and negotiations among the separate units that form established social forces, there must also be affirmed the importance of knowledge of the orientations, classes, and power relationships within a society. In a word, we must affirm the importance of a society's historical experience, directed by values not exclusively embodied in any one of its parts. These values are only realized through the debates and contradictions which give a society life. Class structures are the broken mirror in which society recognizes the simultaneously single and fragmented meaning of its action.

e) . This introductory study can be taken as a useful reaction against illusions that have been entertained about abundance and mass society. At the beginning of French industrialization, Balzac was aware of the money spiral and the breakdown of society, but not until 1848 did the problems of industrial labor and the proletariat come fully to light. In terms of the new society now being organized, are we not at a state comparable to Balzac's time? Western Europe entered the era of mass consumption only ten or fifteen years ago. It is fascinated by the automobile and television and is anxious to enjoy a higher living standard. It is natural that Europeans, once free from the nightmare of crisis and war, at first saw only the heights of abundance and have not yet learned to recognize and express the new social problems. Must we entirely give in to this fascination with the new? Certainly, we must. We must also cease to search, contrary to all the evidence, for the remains of past problems and struggles. We must retain a clear recollection of what European industrialization and the workers' struggles really were. We must not cheapen words loaded with history by speaking on every subject about the working class, the proletariat, misery, and revolution, as if nothing had changed. Above all, we must not be satisfied with the new liberalism which calls for *free consumption* and *free exchange,* as if only the vestiges of the past blocked the road to the future, paved with abundance, good human relations, and "countervailing powers."

It is both true and false that today's conflicts are located more on the level of *consumption* than of production. It is true because this widespread affirmation has the merit of breaking with older styles of analysis and of stressing that private enterprise and accumulation are no longer the central element of the management of the new industrial societies, which are systems of politico-economic decision-making rather than profit- or property-oriented societies. It is false because the defense of consumption does not sufficiently define the socially reforming action of the governed classes.

Extreme forms of today's social contradictions may end in a massive switch of investment and an authoritarian limitation of private consumption for the benefit of the power of the State or the great organizations. However, the technocrats often easily justify their actions by showing that increased production, sooner or later, always brings about a rise in living standards. Consumption can be conceived either as one element of the economic system or as the expression of the freedom of individuals and groups. Therefore, we must oppose to productivity, not consumption in general, but *private life.*

Today, even prosperous citizens risk being subjected to demands which strengthen the power of production; they are susceptible to manipulation by propaganda, advertising, and financial stimulants. They can oppose to these social pressures, not their simple desire to consume more —which leads them to conform to the policy of the managers as well as to oppose it—but their need to maintain a certain unity, a certain ability to foresee developments in their personal life, both in their work and in the whole economic and social system. The tendencies toward mass involvements and toward privatization are, to use the expressions of Edgar Morin,[18] the two complementary and opposed principles upon which the dynamics and social conflicts of advanced industrial societies rest.

Although it is too soon for the new cleavages to be recognized and named and for the weapons of the new social struggles to be defined and discussed consciously and passionately, it is now necessary to attempt to define a new social structure, new conflicts, and new movements. Today, it belongs to the sociologist, as it used to belong to the economist, to write tomorrow's history.

[18] Edgar Morin, *L'esprit du temps* (Paris: Editions Bernard Grasset, 1962).

# II

❦❦❦❦❦❦❦❦❦❦❦❦

# The Student Movement: Crisis and Conflict

The new conditions and effects of economic growth as
well as international tensions and conflicts so completely
monopolized attention following World War II that many
people gradually came to take for granted that our industrial societies, once past the take-off stage, were no longer
subject to great internal social conflicts. Suddenly, student
movements broke out almost simultaneously in many
countries. Sometimes, they do not reach outside the university; in other cases, they trigger more general political
and social crises; in all cases, they hold up to question
more than the functioning of a particular institution—
they question the fundamental choices and exercise of
power in society.

These new movements do not come into being with the

clarity that historical and sociological analysis will one
day give them. They are formed in a period of rapid social
change, and do not, as events, have only one specific meaning. Resistance to change, the breakdown of norms, and
institutional crises affect the action of the social movement itself, that is, the struggle by one historical agent
against one or several adversaries committed to a parallel
and antagonistic effort to gain control of the instruments
and effects of social change. We must patiently separate
the various elements of each event before inquiring into
the nature of its movements, their formation and dynamics.

## Criticism of Over-all Interpretations

In the face of the French student movement that was
both violent and articulate in interpretations of its own
action, the analyst is first of all attracted by two opposing
tendencies. The first one searches beyond opinions and
rationalizations and tries to explain students' unrest by the
crisis of the academic system. Isn't it evident that the
movement found its principal strength in the university
faculties that functioned least well? Many students in the
faculties of letters, especially in the field of the human
sciences, have only vague professional expectations. In addition, the increase in the number of students has only
partially been attended by an increase in the number of
diplomas. The university organization was in crisis because a considerable number of students become dropouts
and because the diploma and the training that the rest of
them receive do not seem to prepare them for professional
roles. These observations are supported if we contrast the

Universities with the so-called "great schools." Students in the classes that are directly preparing for the entrance examinations and, *a fortiori,* students in the professional schools are practically assured both of completing their studies and of finding employment that corresponds to their expectations. For the most part, they remain on the fringe of the movement, using it to modernize their schools rather than participating in its social and political thrust.

This type of explanation quickly reveals its own weaknesses. It is incapable of explaining why and how the movement moved beyond the framework of the university and questioned the whole of society and culture. That this happened in the French experience is evident. Whereas in Germany the phase of the "critical university" was long and active, there was no direct continuity in France between the criticism of the university, led especially by the Sorbonne liberal arts students around 1964–1965, and the crisis of spring 1968. At Nanterre, the phase of the critical university was only an episode that occupied a few days at the end of March and the beginning of April. The determination to emerge from the university, to establish liaison with the militant workers, and to carry on properly political activity quickly took the movement out of the atmosphere in which it began. The population experienced the events of May–June as a general crisis, not as a student revolt.

The second type of analysis tends to identify itself with the consciousness and statements of the involved individuals. The movement then appears to have been carried along by anticapitalist ideology, by the hope for a new society that would be rid not only of the Gaullist regime but of a ruling class which controls society. This type of analysis places great emphasis on the actions of the movement because it is impossible to define the conceptions and program of the students' action. The divergences among the groups are so profound that any attempt to do so is foolish. What common ground is there between the Fédération des Etudiants Révolutionnaires (F.E.R.) and the Jeunesses Communistes Révolutionnaires (J.C.R.), or between Daniel Cohn-Bendit and Jacques Sauvageot? For this reason, it is natural to concentrate on the events and the actions of the movement. That it was, like at Berkeley, a free-speech movement is the essential fact to Michel de Certeau. Claude Lefort emphasizes the rejection of limiting programs and constricting organization. The movement is defined by its capacity to transcend its own objectives, as the helpless professors had observed with bewilderment. (What good was it to negotiate or make concessions? What was demanded with passion seemed to lose all interest for the student movement as soon as it was won.) Very early on, Edgar Morin gave the most general formulation of this type of approach. The movement is defined less by its objectives than by the type of community that it creates. Just as, frequently, the principal function of a strike is to create solidarity among the workers rather than to win a salary increase, so also the student commune is its own reason for being. An antisociety is set up in opposition to the dominant social order. Above and beyond the diversity of ideologies, there was practical agreement on new types of human relations, decision-making, and struggle.

At its limit, this analytical approach is reduced to description. Despite appearances, it inevitably comes back to the approach that it opposes. To define a movement by the movement itself necessarily calls for the type of explanation that we first mentioned. A human group found itself locked into a desperately ill-adapted university organization that was frequently experienced as completely meaningless. This group transformed itself into a primary group whose activity has no significance other than to develop the solidarity of the group and its break with the surrounding society. Can one even speak of a social movement, when a group's action is not defined by its contradiction of an adversary and its subsequent effort to control the entire social arena in which their conflict is situated? Is not the university's loss of its role the reason why the students are reduced to purely self-expressive action, which can be extremely effective in terms of disorganizing the established order by rejection and revolt, but which is caught between disastrous alternatives: rejection either leads to marginality or ends by overturning the social order, but it is impotent in the face of the political problems of governing and directing society.

It is certainly not important that such a movement has no future; its lack of political power does not diminish its historical importance. But the image just outlined impoverishes the observable facts just as much as the first type of interpretation to which it is both related and distant.

It is not true that the May Movement was absorbed in self-expression. The spectacular occupation of the Sorbonne, the proliferation of meetings, speeches, and posters, and the reign of words fascinate the observer, but they are only one aspect of the May Movement. In France, as elsewhere, the student action was not only self-expressive; it defined its adversaries and struggles. In the United States, the movement at Berkeley and Columbia cannot be separated from the struggle against the Vietnam War and the black revolt; in the socialist countries, the student action was part of the struggle against Stalinist or post-Stalinist techno-bureaucracy; so, almost immediately, the major concern in France was the union of students and workers against the Gaullist regime and capitalist society. The Night of the Barricades led to the general strike and the final great battles took place around the Renault factory at Flins. The struggle constantly moved out of the university faculties and developed in the streets, led by students and young workers who were more and more at one with each other. Beyond all the rhetoric, there developed authentic political action that indeed had no program, strategy, or organization, but was deliberately directed against the adversary instead of being turned back on itself to proclaim a student commune. We must recall that the sign of a commune is to create a new power, to make decisions, to appoint and dismiss, to establish laws, government, and justice, while the student movement almost never (with unimportant exceptions) set up any authority. There was talk of self-management in the factories and offices but in the university itself self-management was neither proclaimed nor established. The student movement constantly defined itself by its struggle, without giving in to the illusions of establishing an authority as might have been possible in some of the universities.

These two criticisms lead to two conclusions: In the first place, the student movement is a true social movement, that is, an action carried out by particular social groups in order to take over control of social change. Its objectives and meaning are political and must be understood not in terms of the consciousness of the participants nor of the crisis in the university organization, but in terms of the conflicts and contradictions of society and its social and political system. In the second place, the events do not lend themselves to a single type of explanation: anarchy, revolt, and revolution are all mixed within the chronological and geographic picture.

We must proceed in two stages: first, we must separate the different meanings of the event that are mixed with each other and which it is vain to want to unify in a single, over-all explanation. Then, we must study the dynamics of the movement, that is, the relations and connections among the various aspects that analysis has distinguished. In this way, our study will be largely historical, transformed and enriched by sociological analysis.

## Various Aspects of the Movement

a. *The University Crisis.* The decay of the university is the most visible aspect of the present social crisis. It is also the aspect that is analyzed least well in general terms. The nature and forms of the crisis within the university institution vary very much from one country to another— we will limit ourselves to France. The first thing we notice is the paradox of a university that is in the process of major growth, with the number of students increasing rapidly and buildings being multiplied over a period of ten years, while at the same time its stated objectives and its organization have not been profoundly changed. The old mold was broken under the burden and has not been replaced by a new mold despite a few partial modifications. What explanation is there for this paradox, this growth unaccompanied by development and change in the university system? As strange as it may seem, we do not have analyses and explanations of such an important phenomenon. Let us draw a possible line of analysis.

The renewal of an institutional system seems bound to the conjunction of two opposed forces: the pressure exerted by a new social demand and a powerful capacity for decision-making and organization. An institution, particularly a university, cannot be the direct translation of a movement, but neither is it merely a body of rules and machinery. In France, both during the Napoleonic epoch and in the first decades of the Third Republic, the economic, social, and political rise of new social groups or classes was associated with the power of the State that held a de facto monopoly over university production. In the present period, on the contrary, there is none of that. The political situation guarantees that there will be no collective rise of the working class. It is true that the university has been opened up to new social groups, but this movement is probably no more important than the opposite movement through which the wealthy classes use the university to give their sons and daughters the means—paid for by the entire nation—to protect themselves against the risks of social decline. The ease of many courses and the rapid expansion of the faculties of letters, which are often less demanding of the students, contribute powerfully to increase the university's role as a social parachute. Democratization is far behind growth.

For its part, the State, while capable of setting up great national plans, does not seek to create the means to actively intervene in economic and social life. It struggles along with its bureaucratic traditions. Despite some not negligible efforts at modernization, the Ministry of National Education is an extraordinarily archaic administration, devoid of modern tools of action. Instead of the establishment of a dynamic liaison between the organizing power of the State and a social thrust, we see close relations set up between professional leaders and the administrative bureaucracy. These partners understand each other easily on the subject of growth, which broadens the labor market and bears witness to the vitality and stability of the social system. They experience the greatest difficulty in questioning themselves and even more in inquiring into the new place of the university in the nation. Policy is reduced to management, carried out by a constant give and take among the leaders of the teachers, the unions, and the administrative officials. More than ever, new ideas and accomplishments are relegated to the fringes of the university, particularly to the research bodies.

The crisis of the university is not due to the control of an overly powerful State, but to the actions of a very weak State that is incapable of working out a policy, primarily because it has not been transformed itself by the pressure of new rising social groups. Corporatism and bureaucracy, feeble and often laughable forms of the State's social thrust and its capacity for decision-making, are easily allied in the effort to isolate the university community and thus create the strange situation in which growth is everybody's religion and the maintenance of established rules and interests the common concern.

This decay of the university institution causes more and more violent reactions. The university appears to be a meaningless pole of resistance to social change. On this level of analysis, one cannot yet understand the formation of a social movement. The behavior explained by this analysis would be retreat, indifference, derision, and ritualism. Whether one played the game or not, the university would not be taken seriously.

b. *Rigidity of the Institutions.* This agitation might have become a force for social change and thus have led to reforms. In fact, it did not. Economic growth concentrates attention on consumption, prices, housing, etc. The unions show little interest in university problems which do not yet concern them directly. Access to education seems to them to be a necessary consequence of raising living standards and many wage-earners make preparations to enter their children into educational institutions they respect from a distance, because entrance into them seems to be becoming possible. These social groups are involved in a series of demands that look toward greater participation in the goods of society rather than to a transformation of society. The political independence and secular spirit of many teachers and their organizations have great prestige for the labor union and political forces that concentrate their attacks against the holders of economic and political power. The traditional university involved in its process of growth has almost no enemies on the left. But the students are seen in a bad light by many on that side of things—young unproductive bourgeois, badly organized, intellectual nit-pickers, they awaken more distrust than sympathy. The student movement has no organized ally.

Those who hold political power are simultaneously proud of growth, impotent before the secret games of the bureaucrats and the influential, and deaf to the sounds of the structures cracking up. Neither the most violent labor strikes nor the first waves of the student movement drew their attention. The technocratic world is satisfied with its work and concerned with the most immediate economic problems; it is isolated by the breakup of the old parliamentary forms of representation and the constant concern not to create new forms; it was dominated by the personality of a head of State, de Gaulle, who did not seem ever to have give much attention to the problems of education.

For all these reasons, it was incapable of embarking on social transformation of the university. Its bribes in the form of reforms were aimed only at producing an elite of engineers, experts, and researchers needed for economic growth. For it, society caught between the State and the economy did not exist, except as a troublesome burden whose routines must be made to fall into step with the rapid rhythm of economic change.

The agitation born of the decay of the university system thus led to a clean break, since no institutionalization of social changes and tensions had taken place. This awareness of the break was perhaps more clearly marked among certain teachers than among the students, for the professors had both great facility at making themselves heard and were able to say nothing. All observers have rightly insisted on the rigidity of the university system that hampers its own progressive evolution and fosters the easy spread of discontent and revolt. One of the functions of the present reform is to analyze the university organization, which must both allow initiative and limit explosions.

c. *Birth of an Antitechnocratic Social Movement.* The university crisis and the rigidity of the political and administrative decision-making system explain the agitation, the revolt, and the social disruption. They do not explain the formation of a social movement that, through the university and beyond it, indicted the whole social and political regime. The student movement did not aim at better adaptation to the demands of employment, that is, at the modernization of the university organization. It did not seek to reestablish a decayed order. It simultaneously combated the traditional social function of the university and the education it offered as well as the direction its development was taking. The existence of this movement can be understood only if one grasps the new role of the university in modern societies.

*The university and the forces of production.* The coming of the mass university signifies first of all that students can no longer find places in those professions that are quite limited and are also for the most part on the margin of the economic system: medicine, law, teaching— the three professions that formerly absorbed the great majority of students. Today, these outlets are bypassed in two ways: first, a growing number of students find no place and do not finish their studies, since they are eliminated by progressive selections, the basis of which is never explained; secondly and more importantly, an increasing number of intellectual activities more and more directly influence the production system. Economic growth no longer relies simply on the accumulation of capital and the utilization of a force of manual labor concentrated in industrial plants. Increasingly, it depends on technical progress, research, management methods, and the capacity to foresee and to organize.

Intellectual techniques, in both the natural and human sciences, have developed far enough that university activity can no longer define itself in terms of the transmission of culture and preparation for the "social" professions. Consequently, the new role of the university cannot be separated from a more general economic and social transformation. From the moment that knowledge becomes an essential force of production, the organization of teaching and research also becomes a problem of general policy and the choices made in this area can no longer be governed by respect for traditions or by strictly technical demands.

*Technocracy and its adversaries.* Technocracy does not mean the replacement of political choices by technical choices. Such an idea does not correspond to any type of society and can only suggest a utopia of little importance. No society can reduce ends to means and function without making choices among objectives or, in other words, without the exercise of power. Technocracy is power exercised in the name of the interests of the politico-economic production and decision-making structures, which aim at growth and power and consider society to be only the collection of the social means to be used to achieve growth and to reinforce the ruling structures that control it. On its deepest level, the student movement is antitechnocratic.

Such a movement derives its strength from social forces that are defined by their place within new relations of production and power rather than because they belong to social groups that are either in decline or are relatively far from the centers of decision-making. In the nineteenth century, in a France that was mostly rural, the revolutionary movements were workers movements, because industrial capitalism was the moving force of social and economic change; today, the revolutionary thrust is created in the most modern sectors of economic activity, where the role of knowledge is most important: the advanced industries, centers of research or advanced technology, the universities, information media, etc.

This is not the only current within the university. Growth also increases the economic system's capacity for integration and upward social mobility. The more or less amateur student, sowing his wild oats while he looks forward without impatience to easy entry into middle-class life, has all but disappeared. For an increasing number, the university is the key to entrance into technical, commercial, and civil service officialdom. Many of these students look with favor on any change that will advance them socially. Those groups who were most ready for political action are not in the most professional disciplines but in those where a general intellectual formation and the encounter with acute social problems place the student before the social responsibilities of knowledge, without integrating him into a professional career. In France, as elsewhere, it was mostly students of sociology, philosophy, architecture, and urban studies who questioned the social order.

Because their opposition is directed less against the organization and methods of teaching than against the entire social regime, they immediately seek to carry the struggle beyond the university, even to shed their identification as students. This identification seems to them to be a compromise with the society that would like to use them even while they reject it. Student agitation and revolt become a social movement only when transformed into an appeal for a general, rather than a particular, struggle.

*The students and the working class.* In the United States, Japan, Czechoslovakia, and France, the student movement is not defined by the defense of student interests but by an appeal to the social groups oppressed by the economic and political system. In France, the tradition of social struggles, the weak social integration of the working class as indicated by employer paternalism, the weakness of the unions, and the strength of the Communist Party naturally direct student action toward the working class. Just as formerly the program of the labor movement was the alliance of workers and peasants, so now a new movement, based on intellectual workers, proclaims their necessary union with laborers; but this union is not simple.

The most visible aspect of the May Movement is that this union was realized more deeply in France than in other places. The methods of social management, unemployment among the young, the stagnation of real salaries, and a governmental policy marked particularly by the weakening of the social security system are elements that help explain the coming together of students and workers which, nevertheless, was only accomplished in the heat that followed the Night of the Barricades, under the banner of common opposition to Gaullist power.

The mixture of students and young workers in the street demonstrations or the bypassing of union organizations in some of the companies during the strike must not conceal the essential truth: the mass of the labor movement did not follow the revolutionary thrust of the militant students. It is easy but arbitrary to say that the working class was betrayed by its political and union leaders. The huge communist union, the C.G.T., was partially bypassed, indeed, but by workers who wanted a victory in the style of 1936, a spectacular defeat of the power of the employers, but not a revolution. The plants were not opened to the students. Local C.G.T. officials, who had undertaken a modernization of their union activity, were not at all disposed to join in an action that their central authorities had judged to be adventurist.

Union action was not revolutionary, not through the fault of its leaders but because the center of power is no longer located in industry. It is partly located in an international economic system that influences the French economy because of necessary competitiveness; above all, it lies in the complex system of relations between the great economic groups and the State. For a long time, sociology has felt and expressed this changed situation by replacing the concept of the firm with that of the organization. What used to be called a firm is today an organizational system, a whole complex of productive means, a management structure. The conditions of economic growth are less bound than formerly to the risks and profits of the private entrepreneur. Economic progress means training, scientific and technical research, economic information, land management, the formation and mobilization of savings— mechanisms in which political power plays an essential role, either directly or indirectly.

Labor unionism retains important roles: not only the economic defense of wage-earners, but also the struggle against archaic forms of authority and management, even participation in certain aspects of planning. Increasingly, the workers' interests are particular interests. Unionism is a historical reality inseparable from private enterprise. Because this private enterprise is no longer at the heart of decision-making, unionism is no longer at the heart of the movements for social transformation. These remarks indicate the distance that separates labor unionism from the student movement. They do not mean that the new social movement cannot draw strength from industry. Technocratic power is present there also but unionism can no longer be the privileged bearer of the antitechnocratic movement. The workers take part in the struggle only to the degree that they, like others, are placed in a situation of dependent participation in terms of social change. One may think that many worker groups participated actively in the May Movement; this does not mean that the central figure of the present struggles is the working class, defined in terms of its relation to capitalist property.

*A revolutionary movement.* A social movement is not

necessarily revolutionary by nature. It becomes so only if a class struggle comes up against an institutional system that is unable to deal with the state of production and social relations. Such is the case with the May Movement. Its revolutionary nature resulted from the conjunction of the three elements that we have just distinguished: the decay of the university, the inability of the institutional system to deal with the tensions born of change, and the formation of a new social movement.

The conflict between those who hold economic power and the workers who wish to win social control of growth —its directions, means, and results—takes on a revolutionary form only because the new ruling forces are built simultaneously on the older ruling classes and on rigid institutional defenses. This coming together of the new technocracy, the older bourgeoisie, and the monarchical State, worked out under the Gaullist regime, gave the new social conflicts their revolutionary turn. A revolutionary movement is always the rejection of social, cultural, and political obstacles that protect the old ruling classes and authority, as well as the struggle against new forms of social domination. It does not break out in stagnant situations but in periods of unbalanced economic and social change. In the French situation, one can even say that the crisis of the institutions was clearer than the formation of a new social movement, for the university was still too archaic for its new role as a production force to be a directly experienced reality.

From this resulted the extreme politicalization of this movement, whose political summit was more solid than its social base. Here, we find traits that are quite traditional in French society where social movements tend more visibly to be revolutionary political forces than movements of social transformation. The struggle against Gaullism was a more tangible reality than the assault on capitalism.

The strength of the student movement—and its weakness, as well as its difficulties in getting organized and maintaining continuity in action—came from its direct attack on the centers of power without burdening itself with the defense of any particular economic interests, or with getting involved in the internal struggles of any highly structured organization.

These observations do not claim to analyze any political alliance that might be possible or to measure the chances of any such alliance among the various groups that oppose those presently in power. They only indicate that today's social movement, of which the students are the principal protagonists, is new and corresponds to a profoundly transformed economic system. There is a great difference between the two kinds of analysis, for the new social movement is still very far from having its own political expression. Some elements of the movement, those most influenced by the Leninist tradition, want to organize a new politics. In May, attempts to move in this direction were cut short and had no effect on political developments. New attempts may be made but it is clear that such a new political organization could have only very limited influence for the immediate future. The movement launched by the students is related to the organized political left in the same way as the worker movement during the Second Republic was related to the Parti Républicain. From the point of view of sociological analysis, the novelty of the situation and the social movement is more noteworthy than possible alliances among various elements of the political opposition.

d. *The Cultural Revolt.* The combination of all these

elements does not explain all the aspects of the movement, particularly the ways in which the militants carried out their participation. In this regard, there has been much discussion of cultural revolt and rejection of the consumer society. Such expressions would seem to cover at least three different realities.

In the first place, one can admit that situations marked by rapid change produce reactions in defense of the lifestyles, mental attitudes, and organizational forms threatened by this change. But if such psychological reactions were produced, it is difficult to discover what collective behavior they caused. In nationalist movements, we often see a turning to the cultural past in order to resist externally determined change. The appeal of the past becomes an indirect instrument of a politics directed toward the construction of an independent future. But this "nativism" did not show itself in a movement of urban young people who did not belong to any highly organized social and cultural tradition whose integrity might have been threatened.

In the second place, a social movement in the process of formation—one that has not yet found its place in politics and can more easily proclaim a social break than actually introduce changes—is naturally more "self-expressive" than "pragmatic." Words are the weapons of those who do not have the power to create any properly political strategy. The May Movement did not clash directly with a ruling class but with a society in which the power of the new rulers is largely identified with economic development itself. An opposition movement could only respond to the technocratic utopia, according to which economic growth naturally brings about social progress, with a counter-utopia, the image of a communitarian,

spontaneous, and egalitarian society. This is how the first
anticapitalist movements were formed in the nineteenth
century.

Finally and most importantly, the very nature of the
social conflicts in our programmed society is different from
those in societies during the period of capitalist industrialization. Then, economic power was exercised over labor
and a struggle was organized in economic terms against
unemployment, low salaries, and all forms of economic
exploitation. Today, the workers are not subjected primarily to the law of profits but rather to what is too
gently named the exigencies of change. The centers of
power and decision-making no longer manipulate people
only in their occupational activities but also in their social
relations, their styles of consumption, and the organization of their working lives. Opposition can no longer be
exclusively economic; it is more diversified because those
in power exercise control much more broadly, even though
it is often diffused and sometimes is less directly authoritarian.

A society that is oriented toward a model of change,
rather than a model of order and hierarchy, is necessarily
a society in which the attachment to personal and collective identity is going to be affirmed. This attachment takes
many forms, all the way from the desire for self-direction
to the direct pressures of individualism, sexuality, and
primary groups. The scientific society is also brutal. Resistance to social integration and cultural manipulation ex-
plodes with special intensity among the young, who are not
yet involved in the network of obligations created by massive organizations and in the pressures to maintain living
standards.

The importance of the cultural revolt is that it is both

the mark of a utopian and prepolitical movement and a central and lasting phenomenon connected with the nature of the new social constraints.

## The Dynamics of the Movement

It is not enough to distinguish the various aspects of the May Movement. We must also inquire how they combine with each other in order to determine what forms the movement may take. If a single meaning were assigned to it, it would only be necessary to ask what its strategy was and how it developed and built up to its climax, triumph, or ruin. The impossibility of following such a course best demonstrates the error of every over-all interpretation.

If we begin from the very open analysis that we have just proposed, the study of the social dynamics of the movement is easily organized around one central question: Under what conditions were the reactions to the university crisis transformed into social and political conflict; under what conditions did these reactions, linked with a general cultural revolt, end up creating a relatively isolated atmosphere of rebellion and rejection? Many other combinations of the elements defined above can be envisaged. What is important is not to mechanically construct a typology but rather to grasp the dynamics of a social movement, which, still nascent, can either be transformed into a political force or reduced to a marginal sect.

a. *The Fusion of May.* The importance of the May Movement in France is that student dissatisfaction, manifested by the November 1967 strike at Nanterre or by the incidents a little earlier at Strasbourg or a little later at

Nantes, was rapidly transformed into a social and political movement that affected the whole of French society and awoke echoes in many other countries.

The actions at Nanterre led primarily by Daniel Cohn-Bendit were important because they amalgamated a disorganized but rapidly spreading student agitation movement with ideas of social conflict and cultural revolt embodied in a number of small groups. These had existed for a long time but had not extended their influence very broadly. Some, like the situationists,* held positions that deliberately isolated them from the student world, which they treated with disdain. In contrast, the November strike at Nanterre was primarily marked by a desire for university reform and for student participation in the government of the university system. The accomplishment of the March 22 Movement † was to move student demands far beyond university reforms and at the same time open up the small ideological groups that, like all sects, were locked in doctrinal disputes, the search for purity, and the taste for abstract programs. Once this first step had been taken and the movement was organized, there was a great risk that it would limit itself to self-affirmation and multiply shock tactics and attacks that would lead to nothing but the provocation of greater and greater resistance within the university itself. At that point, the definitive split took place. This was less the doing of the student movement than of the administrative authorities. Starting

* A small intellectual group, which seized the leadership of the Student Union of Strasbourg just to prove its weakness. Some of its writings have had a widespread influence.

† A loose organization created at Nanterre. Its name recalls the first important sit-in in the administration building. Its main leader was Daniel Cohn-Bendit. Anarchists and Trotskyites were the main tendencies among its membership.

from May 3, the movement was drawn forward both by its own broadened range of activities and the simultaneously repressive and hesitant policy of the authorities.

At the outset, no means of expression and political organization were available to link student dissatisfaction to the activities of the revolutionary groups. The university crisis was too profound for the simply reformist movements to be able to carry on any effective action. This was the case at Nanterre when the joint consultation committee made up of an equal number of teachers and students could take no real action because most of the student delegates were too conservative and the majority of the professors too hesitant. No political party had many militant activists in the university, the Union des Etudiants Communistes (U.E.C.) itself having been very much weakened by the withdrawal of its most vigorous elements. Only open conflict, the challenge laid down by the March 22 Movement, and the repressiveness of the administration and the police made possible the formation of a mass movement and the creation of a social crisis that was soon politicized.

All the aspects of the movement that we have distinguished were then melded and they strengthened each other mutually. The movement did not grow from the bottom upward but from the extremities toward the center. Neither the problems growing out of the university crisis nor the political programs of the revolutionary groups drew the greatest attention during May. Rather, it was the formation of a vast social movement that for the first time brought to light the alliance at various points within society of numerous forces which opposed the orientations and power of society.

b. *The Winter Crisis.* The May Movement was revolutionary because it united the affirmation of new social and political forces with the struggle against older institutional obstacles. It struggled against the new society by attacking the old regime, particularly its forms of authority and decision-making. These obstacles still partly remain. French society cannot easily get rid of a bureaucratic system which expresses the incapacity of this society to transform its basic social and cultural orientations. Beyond the personnel role of de Gaulle the conservatism of French society will for a long time create permanent tensions. Even before the death of Alexander, the heirs apparent were maneuvering. Other more specific obstacles have been somewhat weakened. The university system, still both bureaucratic and a closed corporation, is today no longer simply a glob of putty. Perhaps even more important is the evolution of business and industry. It is possible that the unsigned Grenelle agreements * will have more lasting effects than the agreements signed at Matignon in 1936. Whether one views this as progress or setback, greater progress in the institutionalization of labor conflicts was made within a few months than had been made in the preceding thirty years. It is natural that reaction to this development caused an increase in revolutionary groups opposed to the policies of the great central unions; it does not seem to me possible to say that these unions have been seriously weakened.

In sum, the local institutional problems, in the univer-

* Nationwide collective agreements prepared under the chairmanship of the prime minister and agreed upon—but not signed—by unions and employers' associations. The Matignon agreements were signed in 1936, and were considered a great victory by the workers; they introduced paid vacations, the 40-hour week, and the recognition of shop stewards.

sity or in industry, are absorbed, while a political crisis is still possible and, indeed, preoccupies an increasing number of observers, for the empire that wants to be both authoritarian and liberal has more and more difficulty in finding a workable balance. Under the present semi-presidential regime, such a properly political crisis offers a real opportunity for action only to organized political forces that are capable of forming massive coalitions. Assuredly, a political crisis could open a breach into which student or worker elements could flood to change it into revolutionary crisis. This idea influences various groups but these groups will have less possibility tomorrow than they had during May and June to act in a politically decisive fashion.

Consequently, the student movement, while preparing to act in the hypothesis of a political crisis, is actually closed up within the university and is reduced to affirming itself, instead of being led into a broader field of operation, as happened in May. As a result, it tends to split into two tendencies.

The first, which believes in a serious political crisis, wants to replace the spontaneity of May with a concentration of forces, the elaboration of ideology, and political organization. This tendency (which did not succeed in making itself felt during May–June) has reappeared with greater strength during the present phase. It is impossible to evaluate its importance since only such a political crisis would give it strength. The diversity of the groups and their lack of clear ideological orientation lead us to conclude that at least for the immediate future this political organization will be able to achieve only very limited successes.

The second tendency is much less organized and syste-

matic. The expectations and motivations that were aroused
in the spring remain powerful and seek ways to manifest
themselves. Confrontation has been replaced by self-
expression. While a meeting during April at Nanterre
heightened the collective disposition for action, in November or December the sentiments and reactions expressed
without reference to institutions to be fought or changed
could only cancel each other out. Extreme groups, whose
power does not seem to have grown between spring and
autumn, have become more visible, for the simple reason
that the movement as a whole is finding it difficult to rise
above the most elementary collective behavior. Violence,
which with rare exceptions was absent in the university
during May, has appeared in a limited way but enough to
make the difference from May–June clearly discernible.
The political elements of the movement have often tried
with lucidity and even with courage to transform this
agitation into political action. But such transformation
was possible only in two cases: either confrontation would
cause the spread and generalization of the struggle and attack political power—which the isolation of the students
in the autumn made improbable—or the movement would
set itself precise objectives defined in terms of both old and
new institutions. Since this solution was ruled out by a
movement that was determined to maintain a condition of
absolute polarization, whatever political action was undertaken could only fail. The December strike at Nanterre
was a failure: the presence of 3,000 C.R.S.* on the campus
caused no important reactions in the other Paris faculties.
The movement was so weakened that in January the office

* Compagnies républicaines de sécurité, police force, created after the
war to fight communist-led revolutionary strikes and which has played
a central role in the repression of public demonstrations since then.

of the rector could take measures that it would have found very imprudent a few months earlier. It exercised repression simultaneously in several Paris faculties, and at Nanterre at least had recourse to extremely brutal methods. Certainly, there were protests and strikes; some professors occupied the Sorbonne for a night. These responses were not in vain and probably kept the repression from spreading further. But up to the present there has not been any mass movement and we have seen half the teachers of Nanterre congratulate the dean for having been the first to dare loose his police on his students. Many of these teachers would not have dared to publicly rejoice over this a few months before. There was finally a courageous hunger strike, an unusual form of action, which forced the departure of the guards from Nanterre but was not a movement led by specifically political groups. Both the Nanterre orientation and that of the small groups seem to me to be very much weakened. Does this mean that the exhausted movement is going to disappear? I do not think so but I believe that it will develop in several forms that will be less and less organically connected.

The most visible fact is that a movement that began as the work of sociology students is today led by philosophy professors. Vincennes has taken the place of Nanterre, although there is a group at Nanterre similar to, but less important than, the Vincennes group.* The political impotence and lack of organization of the movement are changing it into a movement of intellectuals. Sometimes it is suggested that there be installed into the university itself a revolutionary section in which the definition of knowledge and the means of its transmission would be

* The new university of Vincennes was created in 1968 and built in four months. Many leftist professors and students went there.

determined by political commitment. It makes little difference here whether such an attempt seeks to be recognized for what it is or whether it hides under the mantle
of the traditional organization; it is even unimportant
whether it is a matter of creating a revolutionary university section or only a core of political opposition within the
university. The essential fact is that it is a question of opposition action on the part of intellectual groups, which is
neither the same as the Nanterre spontaneity nor the
spirit of the small ideological groups which had more influence at the Sorbonne. The strength and the "intellec-
tualization" of the movement is that it means a reduction
of opposition and at the same time moves away from social
practice and analysis. There is a risk that the idea of
revolution will be substituted for the formation of a social
movement, and that ideology will take the place of both
political action and scientific knowledge.

Other teachers are very far removed from this fusion of
political involvement and intellectual activity, and distrust its partisan spirit. They attempt with difficulty and
most often as individuals to nourish their scientific work
from their intellectual and active participation in the May
Movement; for them, criticism of the social discussion
is inseparable from more and more demanding scientific
research. They do not behave as revolutionaries but, if I
may use this tired word, as progressives. While those mentioned first are absolutely opposed to the new institutions,
the latter are ready to criticize them, especially from without, to move beyond them rather than ignore them. They
fight against repression and conservatism in the university and for the transformation of the political and labor
union opposition forces, but they reject anything that
might recall, even under a milder form, the brutal op-

position between socialist science and bourgeois science. There is no clear frontier between these two groups: many individuals belong sometimes to one, sometimes to the other. There is, nevertheless, a clear opposition between the two conceptions of intellectual activity; this appears most strongly in the human sciences. There is, in any case, no unity of thought among the teachers who are closest to the May Movement. The S.N.E.S.U.P.* has as much difficulty in defining a policy acceptable to its left wing as it has in defending itself against the Communists and moderates who have taken over its national office.

On the student side, the divisions are clearer. While the Communists were reorganizing, the leadership of the U.N.E.F.† came into conflict with the Action Committees. The effort toward political organization clashed with the will for an absolute split. The elements farthest to the left are trapped in self-affirmation which can lead to spectacular actions but does not attract broad support; at the same time, they remain the most inventive and dynamic force in a situation in which the social movement is unable to express itself or exert any real political influence.

In May, both the struggle against authority and the cultural revolt nourished political action; today they tend to pursue their own directions. That is why there remains lively agitation in the secondary schools; a *lycée* is a much

* Syndicat nationale de l'enseignement supérieur. One of the two university teachers' unions. Generally controlled by the Communists but whose leadership passed to the leftists just before 1968. The Communists regained its control in 1969.

† Union Nationale des Etudiants de France, national students' union, controlled by the leftists. It was weakened and disorganized long before 1968, but was a central participation in the May Movement.

more solid and constraining organization than a university faculty. Cultural revolt changes attitudes and expectations, and transforms various segments of the public and cultural expressions ranging from theater to movies, from songs to dance. Many embers remain from the fire of May, as well as a number of smaller or half hidden fires in various places. The student movement today is deprived of what it had at its inception; it is forced to invent specifically political ideas and objectives under very difficult conditions but its efforts at reflection are today the essential element of the action open to it. The fruitfulness of these efforts will govern the further developments of contestation.

It was quite easy in May to observe the birth of a social movement, the indictment of new forms of power and oppression that are less specifically economic and more social, cultural, and political than in the past. In the middle of the winter, the retreat and fragmentation can foster the belief that we are witnessing the end of a crisis, some final rear-guard battles. It is hardly a contradiction to say that we are witnessing the end of a particular historic event, the May Movement, and the appearance of new forms of opposition and contestation that are more underground (sometimes also more marginal) , which continue to pose problems and to make fundamental conflicts clear. The present crisis of the movement is due to the fact that it is caught between two opposed orientations.

On one side, it can attack a completely contradictory political system that unites new ruling powers in order to maintain old social and cultural models. I do not say that the May Movement was a movement of social and cultural modernization but that a somewhat vague consciousness of new forces, new problems, and new conflicts was activated by its confrontation with a rigid and worm-eaten institutional system.

To the degree that a political crisis still seems possible, it is natural that the movement seeks to accentuate its striking power, its role as the cleaver that broke the political regime, and hopes, one day, to overturn it and to defeat at the same time the economic and social regime. On the other hand, the movement may strengthen itself and make explicit the new social contradictions that account for its revolt and its demands. Until now, the thrust of its opposition has been more "for others" than "for itself." Isn't it necessary to give priority to the analysis of new social problems and to the formation of new forces and new forms of action and to renounce styles of thinking and expression passively taken over from the labor movement of the late nineteenth and early twentieth centuries. The American university movement, because it is more and more related to the movements and problems of today—the black movement, urban disorganization, imperialist wars and interventions—is involved in the creation of social opposition forces that have a much richer future. On the other hand, its capacity for political struggle is much weaker than in France.

It seems impossible for the opposition movement to make a brutal choice for either one of these two ways. An overly clear choice within an ambiguous situation of political uncertainty and social change can lead either to new forms of Blanquism * or, just the opposite, to critical

---

* After Auguste Blanqui (1805–1881) , prominent revolutionary figure, who advocated violent action in the same time as educational reform. His action was directed more toward the underprivileged than toward the working class.

action that is more emotional or even more intellectual than politically effective. Are not this complexity and confusion the mark of French society which is quite modern in terms of the social problems of a post-industrial society and quite archaic in terms of the need to attack the inheritances, obstacles, and constraints of the traditional systems of authority and decision-making.

This is the point of view from which we must consider the apparent disorganization and internal crisis of a movement which can form neither an organization nor a program but which, by its very contradictions, poses the essential problems of society. One historic moment is over; it was defined by the combination of a crisis of change in French society with the new conflicts of a society in which the structures that govern growth subject to their own interests not only the producer but also the consumer, the member of the massive organizations, the city-dweller, and the citizen. The May Movement aggravated the crisis of the State and its institutions but it also unleashed important social changes. The social movement must define itself in terms of its own nature and the nature of its social adversaries as well as of its objectives of over-all transformation, rather than in terms of struggle against models of authority and organization bound to a pre-industrial or bourgeois society, as opposed to modern forms of economic and social power. In May, the struggle against the Gaullist State was a central element of the passage from the student revolt to the general strike. It is possible that tomorrow the on-going movement in the university may not benefit from such a favorable conjunction of forces and may have to discover its own reasons for being, both in theory and in practice. During this phase of incubation, it will live cut off and in isolation, but it will not cease to play its role as revealer of social conflicts and as instrument of the reorganization of the arena in which they are played out.

For the multiple riches of May that have been generously distributed there is now substituted the austerity of winter. Now, one must run the intellectual risk of looking in the apparent disorder and retreat for the broken image of the social movements of tomorrow. It is not a question of waiting for a new May, whose fire was lit on the ridge that separated the old French society from its new forms of activity, organization, and power; in the depths of the new society, tomorrow's history is now being prepared.

## International Comparisons

Rather than directly undertake a comparative analysis of the student movements, we must begin this analysis with the definition of certain dimensions of the student movement and of its situation in society. Several variables can be omitted from the point of view that interests us here, which is inquiring under what conditions student demands are able to indict a social adversary and propose a counter-model of society.

Consequently, I will not take into consideration the elements that define students as a social category; not because this is unimportant but because all the reasons that reinforce their autonomy, that is, their isolation, have been frequently and carefully examined. The weakening of family influence, the lengthening of studies, the formation of vast campuses or student cities, the importance of the young to a consumer market anxious for rapid turnover of products and styles—all contribute to the creation of a milieu that is defined much less than formerly by occupation and work. One can go so far as to speak of a student subculture or youth subculture, and certain movements (the Dutch *provos* and especially English youth) seem at first to express a complete break between youth and society. Such collective reactions can be considered the most elementary forms of the student movement. However, starting from the moment when we consider the student in his professional situation, that is, in the university, we can seek to discover under what conditions dissatisfaction and demands may or may not develop into social conflict and political action.

The special behavior of youth is observed in all the industrialized countries under forms that are often comparable; their similarity is reinforced by the international diffusion of tastes and styles. This special behavior is absorbed into a social movement to varying degrees and in very diverse ways. We must strive to understand the determinants of this absorption, this take-over of a cultural condition by a social action.

It is probably no accident that the countries in which the youth culture is most marked are also those where the student movement has had the least importance to date. It seems to be the case that the same cultural situation which in England took on a strong cultural expression and produced only weak social action, in France is manifested by strong social action and weak cultural inventiveness. The typology being introduced here does not aim at defining different aspects of the student situation but the conditions under which a student movement is formed.

a). The student movement will have different orientations according to whether or not it is formed within an archaic and ill-adapted university system. The first variable to be considered is *archaism-adaptation*. I hypothesize that a social group placed in a crisis situation can rebel and revolt or, on the contrary, can retreat into its traditions and special interests but cannot create action that will transform society.

At the beginning of industrialization, in the first decades of the nineteenth century, there were numerous worker movements, from the Luddites to the Canutes,* which manifested this kind of revolt on the part of the skilled artisans who were mortally wounded by the capitalist organization of production and mechanization. That such movements can be considered the birth of the labor movement is historically acceptable. It remains true, nevertheless, that these worker-artisans by themselves were unable to create the worker movement and that they were in the same situation as the peasants whose economic activity and life-style were destroyed by industrialization and urbanization.

The crisis of most European universities is part of the crisis of a bourgeois culture and society in which class barriers are difficult to break but sometimes decay because of social changes. In the case of the universities, this is especially due to the increase in the number of students, the change in available opportunities, and the influence of agents of socialization and information outside the university institution. Even quite recently, Germany and Italy much more than France still had a university organization directly inherited from the nineteenth century, based on the power of the chair-holding professor, a situation that has no equivalent in France except in the medical schools. Beyond these differences, the European universities on the

* Workers of the silk industry in Lyon. They revolted against the introduction of new machinery and their proletarization.

whole can be considered archaic and resistant to the introduction of subjects, social relations, and organizational
forms required both for their own existence and by social
demand. The American universities—not only in North
America but also in the great Latin American universities
about which it is stylish to speak with disdain—are much
more "open" and are the principal centers of intellectual
innovation as well as organizations capable of almost con-
tinuously transforming their form and activity.

A university institution can be built on an old model
and still not be seriously ill-adapted to the demands made
on it, either because it insures solid professional opportunities or because access to it is protected and it enjoys
great prestige. On the other hand, it is not the more traditional organizations but those under the greatest pressure that run the greatest risk of falling apart and sinking
into a chaos that absorbs discontent instead of helping to
change it into a social movement. In the same way, industries in crisis often have social revolts or strikes but are
rarely the places where a worker movement capable of
far-reaching action is developed.

Only where the universities have a certain modernity (in
relation to the society) can the student movement become
an element of a conflict that affects the directions and
forms of social evolution. We will return later to the
French case that includes elements of modernization if
only through the recent introduction of a reform that
aimed to separate an elite destined for research from the
future middle management, especially teachers, called to
follow a different course. But the faculties of letters that
were the center of the May Movement were still only very
slightly involved in the process of modernization.

b) . The first thing a movement formed in the university

faces is corporative and administrative authorities who are
either capable or incapable of carrying on negotiations.
This capacity, assuredly, depends on the administrative
system and the relative independence of the universities,
but the pressure is often so fierce that institutional rules
are overwhelmed and, consequently, considerable differences appear among the universities of a particular country
or among the faculties of one university. The Paris example shows it: while the deans seemed to be void of all
power to make real decisions and were only able to be
liaison agents between the Ministry of National Education
and their faculties, we must recognize the extreme importance of their role, the diversity of their reactions and
how important these were. Likewise, the role of the rector
of the Technical University of Berlin seems to have been
very important.

Where the organizational system is rigid and incapable
of negotiation, the movement embodying grievances and
revolt has more chance of moving beyond the university
itself and of questioning social power; in the opposite case,
the movement is more likely to stay within the university
institution. We must nevertheless add—something that
applies also to the following paragraph—that at the same
time that institutional rigidity can facilitate the politicalization of the movement, it also reinforces reactions of crisis
and revolt, and leads to greater volatility of action that
may vary wildly from political action to the violence that
betrays confusion of the smallest problems with the greatest, of the most personal with the most general. It has often
been noted that in France, a country of great institutional
rigidity, a mixture of the most petty questions with the
most weighty decisions comes across the desks of the

highest officials of the State. As a result, when conflict
breaks out, one never knows to what degree it is concerned
with these major decisions or is the result of the accumulation of bothersome details that has become insupportable.

Hence, in France, it was not a carefully distilled movement that was moved to political action by institutional
rigidity but, quite the contrary, a complex ideology. It was
a movement aware of conflict, prepared to see society
divided into hostile camps, and skeptical about institu-
tionalizing conflicts that ought to be waged openly. At its
extreme, this institutional rigidity leads to rioting and
civil war; at the least, it very clearly indicates who are the
adversaries facing each other. This situation intensifies
because the resistance of the rulers to negotiation is often
based on their consideration of themselves as the guardians
and defenders of traditions and principles, such as a particular conception of the university, and because they see
themselves above the institution, on the level of general
social forces, such as the opposition between good and evil,
civilization and barbarism.

c). Institutions must not be confused with political
power, that is, with the degree to which the political decision-making system is visible or centralized. What is being questioned here is not the form of political organization but the degree to which the dominant forces and
political power coincide. It is always insufficient analysis
to present the State's power as the direct political expression of the interests of a ruling class. But we can distinguish between situations in which economic and social
change undertaken by a ruling class leads to strict political
control and situations which permit a wide separation between social domination and political power. This variable

can be called the degree of institutionalization of political power; it is weakest when the identification of State organization and economic power is greatest.

Great institutional rigidity can coexist with a movement of economic and cultural transformation carried out by a decentralized alliance of ruling forces not embodied in political elites. Such is the case in Italy. On the other hand, a high degree of university autonomy can be associated with a political system in which the ruling elite plays a highly visible role, which is the case in Mexico and some other Latin American countries and also, it seems to me, in Japan.

When the student movement encounters a strongly established political power, it is led to direct political action; that is, it is led to question the power system. Although the May Movement in France was primarily defined as anticapitalist, at the most dramatic moment of its development it attacked the Gaullist regime as much as the economic power of the large firms and their political agents. On the contrary, a more diversified political system, in which the political elite enjoys less independence and cohesiveness, tends to bring out a more diffuse questioning of the social order, one that is more cultural than political.

Starting from these basic propositions, we can attempt to analyze the real solutions and, even more importantly, define the action-styles of the student movement in the present situation. We will first propose these styles in a relatively systematic manner before reflecting on the general problems of the student movement.

.  .  .

UNIVERSITY ORGANIZATION
(a) ARCHAIC   (b) MODERNIZING

| | | |
|---|---|---|
| Institutional system:<br>1) rigid<br>a) concentrated political power | France | Czechoslovakia |
| b) diffused political power | Italy | Columbia (U.S.A.) |
| Institutional system:<br>2) flexible<br>a) concentrated political power | Japan | Mexico |
| b) diffused political power | Germany | Berkeley (U.S.A.) |

Let us first review the typology:

a) . An extreme case is the situation that combines the elements that lead to strong opposition to the movement with those that lead to the outbreak of revolt against both the university and the whole of society. This revolt is set on the destruction of an archaic system but finds itself unable to emerge from the university in order to overturn society as a whole. The clearest case is Federal (West) Germany. There, the archaism of the university organization and of the authority relationships in the schools is associated with a certain flexibility of the systems of negotiation, especially in industry where powerful unions, through co-management or other arrangements, have brought about a high degree of institutionalization of labor conflicts. Political power is diffused and the role of the political elite is weak, because of the international situation of Germany, the power of the great companies, the association of the two principal political parties in a governmental coalition, and the weakening of the personal role of the Chancellor since the time of Ludwig Erhard.

One is tempted to repeat here the celebrated remarks of Marx on Germany at the beginning of the nineteenth century. Even today, conditions favor the development of theoretical consciousness rather than practical action. Neither in the United States, Italy, or France does one find student leaders possessing the intellectual maturity of a Rudi Dutschke. Only in Germany has the influence of an ideologue, Herbert Marcuse, been so great, while in France Henri Lefebvre, who could have played the same intellectual role, has not done so up to this point. (I am here making the hypothesis that in the present period France tends to resemble the German situation of 1965–1967 because of the new autonomy of the universities, the establishment of bargaining systems, and the conservative reaction of most professors.)

Italy is partly in an analogous situation but the greater rigidity of the institutional machinery pushes the student movement toward broader activity and particularly toward a direct call to organized political forces, either the P.C.I. (Italian Communist Party) or, even more so, the P.S.I.U.P. (a left-wing socialist party). There is semi-politicalization, limited by the nature of Italian political power and by the extreme weakness of the political elite in that country.

b). The Italian situation is in some ways halfway between Germany and France. The only thing it has in common with Germany is the archaism of the university situation. We must recall here that the French university system was less determined on conservative resistance than it was disorganized or even submerged by growth unaccompanied by any real organizational change. Aside from that, everything disposed the French student movement to emerge from the university. Only in France was the stu-

dent revolt able to unleash a general labor strike, the path
to which had been prepared over the two preceding years
by violent strikes, the socially reactionary policies of the
government (cutbacks in the social security system, the
stagnation of real salaries, a propaganda campaign focused
on the sacrifices necessary to insure the "competitiveness"
of French industry when tariffs are supressed within the
Common Market), and above all by the continuing, very
weak institutionalization of labor conflicts along with the
strong influence of the Communist Party. The nature of
the Gaullist regime had two results: the university was
completely unable to negotiate and the movement was
headed toward direct confrontation with the political
power.

Returning to the general terms of our analysis, the
French student movement was better at defining its adversaries and committing itself to action to changing society as a whole than it was at defining or organizing itself.
It was not based on the defense of "modern" interests,
particularly the defense of education against the control
of the technology or political and economic power in
general. Rather, it demonstrated the reactions to the crisis
of an archaic system that was falling apart because of its
own growth. From this resulted the constantly visible tension, indeed the contradiction, between a revolutionary
movement and crisis reactions (the analysis of which is
the central theme of my book on the May Movement).

This situation is quite analogous to the beginnings of
the labor movement in France. I have spoken of the student movement as *utopian communism,* a parallel expression to the term utopian socialism widely used to designate
the intellectual and populist movements of 1830–1848 in
which the negation of the social order and political action

preceded the formation of an organized force to present professional demands. There are comparable elements between the French and Japanese situations and also the Spanish situation. In the first instance, the isolation of the student movement is much greater; in the second, the archaism of the university is so much greater and the forms of social domination are so much more brutal that the Spanish movement is really halfway between those in the industrialized countries and those in the underdeveloped countries. The importance of the movement in France results from the fact that institutional obstacles and political centralization in a situation marked more by university transition than simple archaism brought out a revolt that, in other situations mentioned so far, tends to burn itself out where it starts.

The whole paradox of the May Movement is that, having been launched by the mystic search for a proletarian-revolutionary force and by the struggle against rigid political and institutional systems, it brought to light new opposition forces outside the university (technicians and "professionals" on one side, young workers on the other) and revealed more than anywhere else the nature of a social power until then hidden behind reassuring illusions of modernization, rationalization, and growth.

It is still not an independent, fully developed social movement. It operated more by revealing contradictions than by proposing a "program." It unleashed a revolutionary crisis that is less than a revolution but much more than a crisis of change or adaptation. Here again, there is a striking continuity of national history. The struggle against absolutism determined the revolutionary form of social change in France and the importance of the political and ideological orientations of movements whose summit is more vigorous and better defined than their base. This means that the modernity of the movement cannot be simply opposed to the archaism of the resistance that it met. This archaism played the role of an obstacle that forced the movement to leap higher and further, and thus to reveal new social conflicts and to emerge more deliberately from the limited domain of university problems. If one viewed such movements only as a useless and regrettable crisis, one would miss what is essential, namely the entry onto the historical scene (and into a revolutionary style that is more than opposition) of a social movement of the first importance.

c) . If we turn now to the modern universities, that is, those that are not fundamentally ill-adapted to the demands of society, two extreme possibilities can be envisaged. The first maximizes the chances of a strictly university movement, because the institutional system is flexible and political power is diffused. In this case, the strength and importance of the movement cannot come from its political action, but, on the contrary, from the social revolt that sparks it. This is the situation of the American movement, especially at Berkeley; it is a movement centered on the participants, while the French movement is centered on its objectives. This difference emerges clearly from interviews with the student militants. A young American sociologist who did such work in the two countries was struck by the insistence of the American students on speaking of themselves, their personal history, and the process of their radicalization, while the French students refused to speak in these terms and focused the conversation on directly political issues.

In France, the May Movement provoked a crisis of the regime. The movement at Berkeley and other universities in the United States unleashed a crisis of conscience, while its political expression remained relatively weak. It is even possible that strictly political action against the Vietnam War will not bring about the formation of a lasting political movement any more than the analogous struggle in France by the student unions against the Algerian War. This political current is still only weakly connected with university activity, more on the level of ideas than of practice. The American movement is much more threatened than its French counterpart with remaining a cultural revolt. On the other hand, it is much more capable of developing more inventive social action and of becoming one of the elements within the formation of a movement—not necessarily unified within an organization—to basically criticize society. The difficult relations between the student movement and the black movement seem to me to promise more for the future than the misunderstandings between the student movement and the labor unions in France.

The American situation evokes that of the English labor movement, which is stronger at its base than at its summit, is supported by a strong and specific class consciousness, is engaged in negotiations, and is capable of finding diversified supports on a local level, but also brings out the limited character of a political system of Whigs and Tories, Democrats and Republicans, incapable of expressing the major grievances and demands of the new society. Certainly, one should distinguish—which we cannot do here —different situations within the United States. The source of the principal variations lies in the relative flexibility of the institutions. Berkeley and Columbia are, from this point of view, very far from one another, which can explain the greater violence of the Columbia movement. One would be tempted to say the Berkeley type of student movement is more characteristic of a society in which the universities, as a whole, have a fairly great capacity to negotiate and cope with conflicts.

d). In societies where political power is highly concentrated, especially if this is accompanied by a rigid institutional system, it is the most modern universities that are most likely to see the formation of a specifically political movement different from the North American one. In this case, the student revolt is more directly bound to the formation of a new ruling elite or at least to the struggle against an industrial elite that has become a political bureaucracy and hence a brake on development. To varying degrees in the countries of the East—and preeminently in Czechoslovakia—countries in which the absurdity of the Stalinist system was rendered insupportable by the disappearance of the reserve of peasant manpower, the student movement does not take the form of a movement against the social order, but of action for economic and cultural modernization, and for the realization of a socialist society which the regime is failing to direct.

To this type, we can relate certain aspects of the Latin American student movements and particularly the Mexican case. Here also it is a question of a modern university —a university that is modernizing relative to the present state of society—and of a political system organized around a single party. In Mexico, the university possesses real autonomy that pushes the student movement to develop itself within the university world primarily but also to move toward properly political objectives. Alliance with the workers or the peasants is rendered extremely difficult by the powerful control over these social groups exercised by the internal machinery of the P.R.I.*

This typology cannot be a goal in itself, but only a first step at comparison that takes into consideration the situation of the student movement and its special problems. The remarks we have made lead us toward a more elaborate analysis that is addressed directly to certain of the problems already met in this exposition. They can be summed up in the following way. In theory, we have supposed that a social movement was the expression of a conflict between social forces for the control of social change. In more analytic terms, it is the combination of three elements: the defense of the unity of the action—what we shall call a principle of identity, I; the struggle against a social adversary—the principle of opposition, O; the reference to the whole of society—the principle of totality, T.

There exist rudimentary movements that possess only one of these elements: pressure groups (I), contestation (O), or doctrine (T). There are a good number of partial movements that can be defined as I-T, I-O, or O-T. It is useless to define these more precisely here. The real question is whether there are complete and concrete social movements that combine all three elements in a coherent manner. It seems to me that such a formation supposes an extreme degree of coherence in the social situation and, consequently, an extreme degree of institutionalization of the conflict in question. This may be the case with certain societies like Sweden, in which the power of collective agreements, like the Saltsjöbaden tradition,† and the

* Institutional Revolutionary Party. The official party which has controlled entirely Mexican political life since its creation in 1928.

† The Saltsjöbaden "basic agreement," signed in 1938 between employers (SAF) and the blue-collar trade union (LO), was a landmark in the Swedish industrial relations system.

regular functioning of a parliamentary system assure a very strong relationship of the three points which, together, constitute a social movement. A labor movement like the Central Swedish Labor Organization can act in the name of special interests, that is, the wage-earners, against the interests of the employers and also in the name of economic and social progress.

This means that the conditions that make possible the realization of the theoretical model of the social movement also cause there to be no social movement properly speaking, since conflict is fully institutionalized. This recalls the simpler observation according to which a social movement invents or transforms the situation in which it acts and can never be entirely "conscious and organized." A social movement is always out of balance: its different dimensions—I-T, I-O, O-T—never match perfectly.

We recall Lenin's criticism of economism and trade unionism and the opposite distinction made by Selig Perlman between the desire for "job control" on the part of the workers and the political orientation given to the union movement by intellectuals. Such observations can be generalized and separated from their ideological content; they demonstrate that it is in the nature of social movements not to be able to be integrated and unified. To speak more concretely, professional defense, social struggle, and political program are always more or less dissociated. The diversity of the situations considered should not then lead one only to distinguish movements according to their content but to distinguish them more profoundly on the basis of the relations among their elements.

The simplest thing is to define a movement by that element that plays the most conspicuous role, the element that is ahead of the others. Thus, in Czechoslovakia, it is the O-T element, the criticism of power in the name of a model of societal development; in the United States, it is the I-T element, a group-centered revolt against the social order; in France, during May, it was the element of struggle, I-O, that led the others. In each instance, internal imbalances are produced within the movement which in their turn bring about the production of ideologies whose function is to affirm coherence among elements that in fact are noncoherent. From here we can return to the analysis of the situations themselves.

In a situation marked by liberal growth, in which the *Enrichissez vous* (Get rich yourselves) of the July Monarchy or the Victorian era dominates, conflicts among social forces are retarded relative to an over-all reaction in terms of the society and its culture. On the other hand, in a situation marked by highly managed development in which the role of the State is very visible, the element O-T moves ahead of the others. The conditions that give priority to the I-O element, that is, the most concretely conflictual element, are probably more difficult to determine and may correspond to a situation that combines the visible role of the State with strong liberal growth, as in the case of France.

In each situation one must start from the main impulse of the movement in order to understand both the movement's action and the internal difficulties it meets. Let us emphasize that this approach is quite different from that—highly criticizable in our opinion—which begins with an abstract model of progressive, controlled, and institutionalized change and conceives social movements only as reactions to the obstacles opposed to this progressive change and therefore in themselves signs of disorder, not agents of social transformation. It could be objected that student movements are not part of the most rigid institutional systems. But it seems to me that such a point of view confuses two orders of problems: the functioning of the social system and the questioning of the directions and power that characterize a society. In the functioning of institutions, one could say that their rigidity causes clashes, revolts, and crises—but this amounts to a tautology.

Jessie Pitts has brilliantly developed these ideas in terms of France, where authoritarianism has delinquency and bawdiness as its counterpart. This is quite exact on the level of the behavior of individuals and collectivities defined by their place within an organization. But one must add that this kind of institution gives political importance and responsibility to the opponents of the social and cultural system. On the other hand, in a more decentralized and empirical society, opposition may be embodied in retreat or deviance. Where the I-T element is strongest and cultural revolt is stronger than social conflict, it is more difficult for the rejection of values and norms to be transformed into a movement capable of changing the social order. In the opposite way, institutional rigidity, while favoring a generalization of grievances and dissatisfactions, turns away from real politicalization and expresses a crisis more than it provokes a social movement. If we generalize these observations, we move away from the simple construction of a typology toward the following idea.

Each of the three types that we have just defined by the predominance of one of the dimensions of a social movement questions the social order. None can be considered purely as reaction to a crisis situation. They all carry their action well beyond immediate demands; they all seek to embody social and cultural contestation rather than institutional regulation of conflict. At the same time, each of these types is threatened by a double internal contradiction, which opposes its strong element to each of its weak elements.

In the French case, defined by the strength of the I-O dimension, there are also political weakness and weak participation at the base of the movement. The first fact is apparent when one listens to the violent arguments between the leftist students and the leaders of the Communist Party and the C.G.T.* These speak in terms of the possibilities of a political solution of the crisis and accuse the *"enragés"* of having sabotaged their work to install a leftist coalition government. The second condition caused the rapid passage from action led by very limited groups, the so-called "little groups," to a mass action which was mobilized only by the police repression and the crisis that followed.

In the Czechoslovak case, the political effectiveness and importance of the movement were combined with incapacity to define a properly social conflict and difficulty in according great importance to the cultural revolt. The student movement is a political detonator and has no great capacity for independent action. Finally, the American-type movement, in which the cultural revolt is very much marked by political rejection, remains locked into this revolt and experiences the greatest difficulty in setting social content and political objectives for itself. We could add that a movement of the German type, which is primarily revolt and negation, fails to establish itself forcefully in the cultural order, the social order, and in the

---

* Confederation générale du travail, the biggest communist-led, French trade union.

political order, and tends consequently to replace flagging action with powerful ideology. Ideology fills out the weak dimensions of a movement.

The French imagined a self-governing and spontaneous utopia stopping the two gaps in their movement: professional organization and political objectives. The Czechs and those like them invent a reconciliation between socialism and liberty that is more an ideological construction than a political program. The American students totally reject their society, which dispenses them from analyzing its social conflicts and seeking forms of political organization. But these weaknesses and ideologies are also the moving force of the movements. They will be reduced only to the degree that new social conflicts will build up, be organized, and, subsequently, be institutionalized.

The principal task of a dynamic study of the movements is to consider how these unbalanced, contradictory, but powerful uprisings are changed into balanced, organized social forces which have lost their capacity to transform the social order. A social movement is not an idea, a program, or a doctrine. It does not oppose a rational and balanced solution to the contradictions of a society. Only doctrinaire utopians are attached to the creation of such a model of the ideal society. A social movement deserves the name only because of the contradictions within it and the imbalances that thrust it forward. Even when it is apparently conscious and organized, it lives only on its discords and internal struggles. The greatest weakness of today's student movements is their illusion that they can live their objectives and can construct and consummate an antisociety. The importance of the May Movement in France does not at all reside in the lyrical illusion of the occupied Sorbonne; the electric arc does not produce electricity; it uses it. Its importance resides in the study of the contradictions that oppose political intention, social struggle, and cultural revolt. If the March 22 Movement was at the heart of the movement, the reason is that it was both libertarian and socialist, because it lived the union and contradiction between the red flag and the black flag.

The history of a social movement is always a long effort to move beyond its internal contradictions and thus arrive at its realization and consequent disappearance. No one can foresee to what degree and under what conditions the student movement will be destroyed by its internal problems or will dominate them powerfully enough to extend its action and influence. But we can say that the measure of this success or failure is the capacity of the student movement to participate in a social and political action that transcends the university and assures the convergence of students and other groups of the opposition.

This is perhaps where an international comparison ought to begin today. Instead of placing at the center of the analysis the general aspects of the student situation, it should emphasize the study of the formation (or the nonformation) of a social movement and consequently consider with the greatest attention the passage—willed by the student movements themselves—from university revolt to more general battles carried out in alliance with other social forces.

# III

❦❦❦❦❦❦❦❦❦❦❦❦❦

# The Firm:
# Power, Institution,
# and Organization

## The Sociology of the Firm

In the countries that experienced capitalist industrialization, the great independence of economic institutions in the nineteeth century brought about a division of two academic areas: to the economist was assigned the study of the firm and production or exchange; to social thought and later to sociology was assigned the study of working life, of attitudes toward work, and of the social relations within firms. When one speaks of the social problems of industry, it is clear to almost everyone that this means primarily the life and work of the workers and, secondarily, of other wage-earners. Still, it is necessary to distinguish two stages in the evolution of the work and in the process by which the social problems of industrial labor were taken into consideration.

During the first stage, the worker appeared almost exclusively as one who carried out a task, because production faced few problems other than those concerned with economic management and technical manufacture. Since the workers exerted no influence over economic management, their role was purely functional. Whether skilled or unskilled workers, whether their professional independence was great or minimal, it was not necessary in practice to take into consideration the internal social problems of firms. At the most, liberal ideologues wanted the systems of remuneration to become capable of giving the workers a merchant's mentality. Public opinion, philanthropists, and reformers were far more aware of the workers' misery, of the problems created by the formation of great urban and industrial concentrations, the exploitation of female and child labor, and the consequences of uprooting, social disorganization, and economic exploitation.

A second stage opened with the beginnings of the organization of work, that is, with the appearance of *social rationalization*. With the formation of great mechanized enterprises, the study not only of machines but now of factories led to the realization that the effectiveness of an enterprise depends in great part on its efficiency as an organization. The results of manufacturing appeared more and more to be governed by the effects of the administration of the enterprise. Attention was directed to the workers' reaction to work, and Taylor, not first but more vigorously than most, recognized the importance of "slowing down" and strove to suppress this obstacle by the use of financial stimulants. After Taylor, the recognition of the frequent failure of this type of manipulation led to the recognition of the existence of collective "feelings" and informal, rather than official, norms of production, of the importance of the type of leadership on the results of the working group, etc.[1] In a parallel manner, the role of the executive as organizer was the object of numerous studies and the work of Chester Barnard[2] established the connection between the ideas of Mayo on worker behavior and the study of executives. The "human relations" school abundantly developed these themes, studying the psychological conditions requisite for good communications within a firm.

This conception of the industrial enterprise is now widely attacked. The attacks come from two sources that are more opposed than complementary. They must not be confused.

a). The study of the behavior of employees, and of manual workers in particular, has rightly recalled that workers are placed more in confrontation with the firm than within it. Their desire for participation is limited by the need to defend their personal interests. Certain decisions must be made: to remain in the company or look for another job, to push production (when the worker is able to vary his output) or to limit the intervention of the organizers. That social policy and the climate of the company act as determinants of these choices does not stop them from being able to be understood as the expression of the particular role occupied in the firm. Chris Argyris[3]

[1] This development has been set out very well by Reinhard Bendix, *Work and Authority in Industry* (New York: Wiley, 1956), and by Bernard Mottez, *L'evolution des systemes de remuneration. Essai sur les ideologies patronales* (Paris: CNRS, 1967).

[2] Chester I. Barnard, *The Functions of the Executive* (Cambridge, Mass.: Harvard University Press, 1938).

[3] Chris Argyris, *Personality and Organizations: The Conflict Between the System and the Individual* (New York: Harper and Row, 1957).

has especially insisted on the complex personality and organizational relationships; a French study [4] tried to explain worker behavior based on the type of "project" in which the worker is involved. Another study [5] that particularly considered workers from agricultural backgrounds demonstrated that they were primarily motivated by a desire for upward social mobility and that they most often considered their situation within the firm only in terms of their plans for social advancement. One might speak of these workers as marginally integrated for they did not feel part of the firm or of the working class, and their satisfaction or dissatisfaction was determined by whether they were conscious of progressing toward the goals they had set themselves.

If we consider non-economic organizations, like research laboratories, we can see an opposition between the researchers who define themselves by membership in a team or a school and those who oppose to this idea of social integration personal objectives that may concern both their professional careers and their intellectual creativity. A "human relations" policy that aims at better integration of the whole group risks favoring conformism and weakening the organization by ignoring the personal "interests" of its members.

In a parallel manner, one could reproach this old conception of the organization with deliberately ignoring the necessity to adapt itself to a changing environment, whether of the market or of some other aspect of its activity. A firm must be organized in terms of its objec-

[4] René Bassoul, Pierre Bernard, and Alain Touraine, "Retrait, conflit, participation," *Sociologie du travail* (Oct.–Dec. 1960) : 314–329.

[5] Orietta Ragazzi and Alain Touraine, *Ouviers d'origine agricole* (Paris: Editions du Seuil, 1961) .

tives [6] not its balance and integration. It has a game to play; it does not control the conditions under which it must act and so must make its decisions in terms of what changes its partners may be able to effect. At the upmost, the industrial enterprise no longer appears to be a social system and collectivity but a system of relations between external and internal demands, hence an instrument for negotiation and choice that possesses no constant content, no system of norms, roles, and status that stably define the conditions of its balance.

b). On the other hand, the firm can be conceived as a political unity. That was already the conclusion of Berle and Means following their classic study of the decision-making system in the great American corporations. In entrepreneurial capitalism, the model in the development rests on the notions of risk, profit, and market. This defines a certain state of economic and social organization but not the internal values of the organization. From the moment that growth appears to be more defined by the capacity to combine in long-term programs either ready resources or resources to be created or developed, the whole organization is seen to be subjected to the objectives of development which are the business of the whole of society. The massive organization—whether it is industrial, commercial, medical, or university—carries in itself the rationalizing model that orients its social activity. To modernize, rationalize, and program appears as the fundamental exigency starting from which social policies are to be defined.

The more one considers the firm as a society, the more

[6] Tom Burns and G. M. Stalker, *The Management of Innovation* (London: Tavistock Publications, 1961).

one is also led to bring to light the power conflicts that develop in it, whose object is the social control of the rationalizing model. The firm is an instrument for development, but how is this to be defined? In practice, social demands are referred more and more to the objectives of growth. Does not union pressure oblige the ownership to search for better productivity by a rationalization of decisions and organization which questions the established more and more closely connected to the economic developed the idea that within the modern industry the political objectives of the labor movement should be more and more closely connected to the economic demands of the workers. It is a question of transforming economic growth into social development and of attacking the power of the managers. Considered on this level, the firm is defined by the relations of rationalization and politics.

The firm is organized rationally. Not only does it adapt its means to the objectives and to the incessant changes in the situation in which it acts, but it strives to attain a rational end, the best possible utilization of its human, technical, and financial means. But it can attain this end by defending its particular interests and this defense takes place both in terms of the means and the end. Consequently, to simply distinguish the organizational level from the political level of the firm seems insufficient. Without renouncing this distinction, we must first of all emphasize that a firm is a particular agent. If it pursues only private ends, it has no institutional function, but neither will it have any organizational solidarity. If it pursues only public ends, it is no longer a real enterprise but only a production facility servicing society. Today, it does not seem possible to maintain that such a situation entirely favors economic rationality. Quite the contrary, because such extreme politicalization brings about the absolute extreme of rigidity, it becomes impossible to separate rationalization from politics, unless one admits the hypothesis of a political system entirely governed by rationality—the technocratic ideology. This is the point of departure of a sociology of the firm: *a private institution fulfilling a social function; an intention of rationality carried out by a private political system.*

The firm is a private institution to the degree that it is not a bureaucratic system in Weber's sense of this term. But it ceases to be an institution if either the managers or the wage-earners do not establish a bond between defense of their own interests and pursuit of ends recognized as legitimate by society. The object of a sociology of the firm is to research how these ends are pursued through the private relationships of labor.

If one considers a unit of production as an organization, one must call on the body of concepts elaborated by the analysis of social systems. One must first define status and roles, then the basic units of social relations, the relation between the role and the expectations implied by a role. Then proceeding through the progressive broadening of systems of social relations, one must study primary groups, groups with formal organization, and communication systems. At the same time, the individuals involved will be defined more and more broadly, taking into account their different levels and the varying ways in which they belong to the system or are related to it.

The study of firms as institutions must refer back to different notions. The whole production network and its internal system of social relations is not the focus of the analysis, but rather the contradictory direction of the societal values of various groups. One must place oneself within the viewpoint of the involved individuals and define for each of them the three fundamental elements of an action system; namely, a principle of defense or identity, a principle of opposition, and a principle of totality. Each of the individuals is related to general values—but only in terms of the contradiction between the defense of private interests and opposition to other private interests. What is here called the principle of totality is not an explicit reference to societal values. These are only indirectly focused on, through the conflict of interests which defines the area of the conflict.

The field of action thus defined has no unity of its own. It is not organized around values and norms. The individual "projects" of those involved in this field are related to each other in terms of reciprocity. This obligates them to both an effort to define the structure of this field of action and to the recognition of the possibility of negotiations through which these programs may be adjusted to each other. Study of the firm is always two-fold. It can be satisfied with neither the image of a common task in which partners collaborate nor with that of absolute conflict over private appropriation of the material products of economic activity for the benefit of managers, wage-earners, or the State. The study of the collective relations of work—often called industrial relations—cannot be separated from the study of the orientations of this activity; nor can it be absorbed into it. The tension that always exists between the structural study of an action system and the analysis of industrial relations is the direct expression of the contradictory nature of the firm as a private institution.

At the end of these analyses, the firm no longer appears

as an organizational or social system but as an agency that functions on several levels. For this reason, the firm is not a sociological concept but a social reality that analysis must take apart. There is no more theoretical unity among the various elements of the firm than there is a unified system of the attitudes toward work. The notions that have been so often used in the past to draw together the observations of industrial psychosociology—satisfaction in one's work and the morale of the firm—have no scientific justification and clumsily disguise ideological choices.

Workers act simultaneously in terms of their own interests, their status, their roles in the organization, and the power conflicts in which they are involved. The essential concern of industrial psychosociology, which is the study of attitudes toward work, consists in researching what determines the relations between these three levels of conduct. In the same way, the sociology of firms must inquire into the relations between strategy, balance, and the politics of the firm. This presupposes that one recognize the specific character of each of these levels of analysis, each of which requires a particular set of analytical tools. It is pointless to present an over-all view of the social problems of industry in terms of market, strategy, or the social system—or even in terms of class struggle.

The union movement, like industry itself, exists on the three levels that have just been distinguished and is well acquainted in practice with the necessity and difficulty of relating them to each other. Union demands most often concern the defense of special interests, increasing advantages, and lessening costs to the greatest degree possible. But trade union policy that is purely concerned with demands and self-defense is quite rare. Union action also takes place on the level of the organizational system and is concerned with the norms and forms of authority within the company. It seeks to increase the participation of wage-earners in decision-making and in the organizational setup that determines their working situation. Finally, we customarily speak of the labor movement only to the degree that the union organization acts, directly or through the intermediary of political parties, in order to change power relationships and the social control of economic change. Shop stewards cannot act only on the level of political struggle; neither can they confuse themselves with the members of the plant committee. Union organizations are usually very careful to guard freedom of movement and not to be locked into a limited system of worker participation.

Within the industrial company itself, there are analogous tensions among these three levels. There is no continuous passage from the level of carrying out the work to the level of organization and from this level to that of management; each has its own unity and system, marked off by defined frontiers and working guidelines. The distance that separates the workers who perform their tasks from the staff of the organization or bureaus has been strongly resented for a long time. More recent is the distance that has been created between the organizers and those in management positions and between the middle-rank staff and the other managers. But this discontinuity must not be confused with class situations, which are not in a position on a hierarchical line but are defined by conflicts over power.

The transformation of industry and, consequently, the evolution of the conceptions of the industrial company can be analyzed as the progressive appearance of organization and institutional mediations between economic power and professional activity. In the old industrial company, economic power and professional activity were separated into the world of capital and the world of labor. Capital exercised direct power over labor. The combination of workers in the capitalist factory permitted the holder of economic power to accumulate capital. The industrial company was more than a market; it was the place where capital was exalted over labor. This can be represented by a simple schema:

Economic power

---

Productive work

In a second stage, there appeared the organization of work and, indeed, the very concept of organization. Economic power was exercised over labor through organization, which also had a certain autonomy that allowed the application of such concepts as status, role, stratification, authority, integration, or marginality, etc. This is represented by the following schema:

Economic power

---

Organization

---

Productive work

The plant manager was no longer just the representative of the capitalist; he was also the one who directs, co-ordinates, integrates, and maintains the organization. In a third stage, economic power moves a step further away from direct domination of productive work. It is no longer only the accumulation of capital and managerial capacity that determines growth; more and more, it is a whole complex of action purposely directed toward growth and the creation of new forms of productivity and efficiency in the economic system. The rulers of economic production participate in these actions and in this sense they are technocrats. At its limit, however, this situation destroys the notion of the firm and replaces it with the idea of the economic system.

Nevertheless, the firm remains—and not only as a unit of production and as an organization. It is also an autonomous center of decisions, whose action is embodied not only in a concerted and general action of growth but must also calculate its particular interests in terms of other units of decision-making and in terms of the incessant changes that affect its activity. It must also negotiate with all the elements within it that seek to intervene in its decisions. This intermediate level between the economic system and the organization I call the institutional level. We come then to the following schema:

Economic power
_____

Institution
_____

Organization
_____

Operations

We must now consider the relations among the elements of analysis that have just been distinguished. Three themes will be presented in succession: *1*) Industrial evolution brings about a growing reinforcement of the highest levels within the firm. The decline of professional autonomy brings about first the control of the execution of work by the organization and then the control of the organization by politics. *2*) In a parallel manner, the independence of each of the levels develops in such a way that their hierarchical arrangement presents itself as the fitting together of subsystems, each of which maintains its own independence. 3) Relations between these tendencies—the hierarchization and growing autonomy of the subsystems—depends on the type of industrial society under consideration. The type is defined along an axis running from liberalism to voluntarism.

## The Evolution of the Firm

The general principles that have just been introduced must be applied historically. There is a simple hypothesis that can guide this analysis: throughout the evolution, the modern firm tends to be increasingly directly defined as a political system that governs technical and economic rationality. By industrial society we mean every society that defines its institutional system as a means of social control over economic development. This type of society apprehends itself as the child of its works and as economic policy. This does not mean that all social life can be reduced to this dialectical relation between development and democracy, but only that the principles of legitimacy on which societal decisions rest cannot be defined outside the relation that joins production and its social utilization. An industrial society, like its firms, is no longer legitimate if it breaks this relationship, or if it does not assign value to its own development—a situation, nevertheless, that is quite frequent, particularly when inflation constrains various social groups to demand the maintenance of a standard of living or the protection of the privileged situation they have acquired. Social groups are likewise engaged in an illegitimate action when, becoming involved in collective, descending social mobility, they are moved only by a desire to regain a lost situation and are thus led to defend an anti-rational vision of society, as the liberal middle classes often do when they are failing.

To again take up the terms used above, the evolution of the firm leads to a greater and greater integration of industrial relations in the politics of the firm, at least to the degree that they concern the institutional rather than the organizational functioning of the firm. More generally, it leads the participants to define themselves more and more by their relations with others and no longer by their possession of specific qualities or absolute rights which are in principle incompatible with the attributes and rights of other participants and which leave no room for a true system of social relations.

a). The stages of this evolution are not measured by chronological units but rather by the existence of what can be called rationalizing models. Since a firm is a complex of administrative instruments that allows passage from economic policy to technical execution, it is easy to distinguish three theoretical stages in the progressive penetration of rationalization. It was first applied only to the area of execution and was a matter of *technical rationalization,* the work of technicians (among whom must often be included skilled workers). It next penetrated into the area of administration or organization, becoming *organizational rationalization.* Finally it reaches the level of decision-making, creating a triumph of rationality; but that rationalization becomes the arena of social conflicts in the firm and in industrial society.

The first stage of this evolution is defined by a very limited application of rationalizing models. The organization and management of firms remained dominated by capitalist profit, although manufacturing workers often possessed great professional autonomy. Their union activity within the firm could only be defensive and their desire to control economic life could only be manifested outside the firm by specifically political means, whether violent or not. This separation of union defense from political action was as clear in the revolutionary unionism of the Amiens charter as it was in so unrevolutionary a movement as the American Federation of Labor. Within the firm, the problems of organizing work had no independent existence; job defense and economic exploitation faced each other. Systems of remuneration based on personal output or on piecework demonstrated this direct conflict between labor and capital. Supervisory personnel and staff employees were only the instruments of capitalist power, charged with imposing discipline and assuring output.

At this stage, the firm is an economic unit, a labor market. The development of professional independence, capitalist domination, and political action are all very much separated from each other. When one speaks of the social problems within this kind of firm, one immediately thinks of the working and living conditions of the workers, not of the functioning of the firm as an organizational and decision-making system. Likewise, the economic analysis of the firm does not bring in the internal relationships of work; it primarily suggests a terminology of the market. Beyond its role as guardian of the dominant economic interests, political life appears foreign to the social struggles that are supposedly waged in strictly economic terms. The firm is where classes confront one another—classes defined not only by their relation within the process of production but as real groups with real heritages, socio-cultural as well as economic.

As Schumpeter has emphasized both in *Capitalism, Socialism and Democracy* and in his essay on social classes,[7] the rationalizing of the entrepreneurs is inseparable from their attachment to such anti-rationalist values as the family, the transmission of acquired goods, class barriers: "The capitalist regime is not only based on supports made up from non-capitalist materials but even derives its driving force from non-capitalist rules of conduct that it is simultaneously condemned to destroy." The conflict between rationalization and accumulation demonstrates the absence of an economic and social policy based on rationalization, which is affirmed only on the level of labor and instrumentality.

In a similar manner, the workers enclose themselves in defense of their trades or working power. Both employees and wage-earners identify their private interests with the general interest, dreaming of a harmonious society in which everybody would act as they do—a market-society or a cooperative-society. They understand each other enough to refuse all autonomy to the institutions of society, particularly the State. In default of a world composed entirely of entrepreneurs or workers, they wish only for a world dominated by the direct relations—peaceful or violent—between employers and wage-earners.

b) . When the rationalizing models reached the level of the administration of firms—a movement known at its beginnings as the scientific organization of work—

---

[7] Joseph Schumpeter, *Capitalism, Socialism and Democracy* (London: Allen and Unwin, 1942) ; *Social Classes in an Ethnically Homogeneous Environment* (New York: Meridian Books, 1951) .

employers and wage-earners began to define themselves by their roles within a social system. On the workers' side, the notions of craft and working force gave way to those of skill and output. On the side of the employers, the idea of the head of the firm replaced that of the entrepreneur. Private initiative and risk were combined with the capacity to transform a production apparatus, not merely to make it function. Schumpeter places at the center of the owner's function at this stage the role of "creative destruction," the capacity to destroy some investments in order to realize others. Henry Ford is often taken as an example both of those who knew at the given moment how to revolutionize production and who then (in 1925–1927) resisted development, while General Motors, under the leadership of A. Sloan, knew how to adapt itself to changes in the market. The American corporations are the best example of those massive organizations that remain politically oriented through the search for private profit. If C. Wright Mills' ambitious thesis of the power elite [8] can only be accepted with great reservations, one can more easily admit his category of the "corporate rich," a fusion between the managers of the massive organizations and the capitalist interests that control them. Sloan, for example, took over the management of General Motors, born as the private work of an entrepreneur, Durant, after it had passed under the control of DuPont, following financial difficulties. The great industrial empires, like U.S. Steel and Vereinigte Stahlwerke, are simultaneously great rationalized organizations and the constructions of financial capital whose existence was not justified simply by economic rationality.

[8] C. Wright Mills, *The Power Elite* (New York: Oxford University Press, 1956).

In this situation, the workers defended their interests in the firm in the name of a society dominated by class conflict. The idea of class struggle itself manifests the recognition of a society understood in its totality as a system of production and no longer only as the projection of the interests of a social group. But this unity of industrial society is introduced only indirectly, that is, by being denied and through the explosion that the class conflict forces on it. The State regained some autonomy, because it arbitrated social struggles or generalized them.

The head of the firm no longer spoke in the name of his own initiative or capital, but in the name of his firm. He fought all interference from outside forces—the State and its social laws particularly—that could create a rigidity harmful to the dynamism of the firm and the economy. In this situation, the firm appeared cut in two. On one side, it is a social organization, on the other, a center of economic decision-making. If it calls on sociology, it wants it to study the workers, the departments, or the staff, not the government of the firm.

The themes of bureaucracy and human relations respond to and complete each other. The social reality of the firm is conceived as a system of rules and relations. The decline of professional autonomy, the fact that craft is replaced by status and roles would lead to an analysis, based not on real social groups, but on work relationships within a system defined by values, norms, and forms of authority and balance. The internal problems of the social organization begin to be treated by new bodies which, even though purely consultative, can intervene very effectively to transform the social management of the firms. What has often been called workers' participation in management is in reality only the intervention of personnel officers in this social administration, without the centers of economic decision-making being affected in any way by this participation.

c). This two-fold nature of the firm tends to disappear to the degree that economic growth comes to depend more on the capacity to mobilize and organize resources, to direct change, and to foresee and program development, rather than on merely putting profits—valued more highly than directly productive work—at the disposal of the entrepreneur. At this stage, the efficiency of the firm depends more and more on social and political determinants and on the general functioning of the economic system, which extends itself to all aspects of social life: use of land, professional training, investments in research, etc. On the level of the firm, economic policies may be formalized into decision-making systems, while the "options" that determine the directions of economic and social change are on a higher level.

This evolution may either reduce the firm to a subordinate role of putting into practice policies decided on a higher level or it may associate the firm with a system of economic and political cooperation. It is the financial and industrial groups, national and international, rather than firms as such that participate in the working-out of economic policy. In all cases, the decision-making capacity of the firm is no longer defined by its situation in a market but by its penetration into a political system.

This penetration has often been conceived as bringing about the disappearance of the private firm. Only the socialization of the units of production has seemed, to Schumpeter for example, to allow the completion of the rationalizing work undertaken by capitalism, which it cannot complete because of the hostility that it has created against itself and because of the fundamental bond it maintains between economic rationality and pre-industrial values. Today, this conception appears too rigorous, particularly because an entirely public firm risks losing its flexibility in terms of decision-making and because political imperatives can come into conflict with the demands of rationality.

Whatever institutional solution may be chosen, it appears that an industrial society, because it is by its very definition a dialectic between development and democracy, rationality and politics, supposes that the centers of economic decision-making and of political intervention enjoy some practical autonomy. It is necessary, as a result, to recognize the existence of private economic institutions, which are the work neither of entrepreneurs nor of "corporations" and which are rationally organized and subject to the motive of private profit.

In this situation, the managers of the firm become a political power, in the sense that their action aims directly at economic rationality and strives at the same time to direct the social utilization of the products of collective labor. This political power can cause conflict with the demands of the workers, or more exactly of the consumers. Such is the meaning of the technocratic threat. It is absurd to speak of the power of the technicians as if authority over execution or even over administration could be substituted for political power and dissolve the ends in the means. The reign of the engineers or even of the scientists has been conceived by some imaginative spirits; it represents a contradiction in terms and no historical example has ever given the least real image of it. If it happens more and more often that the technicians rebel against the power of the financiers, this is anachronistic; these revolts have never led to an effort by the technicians to take over the power themselves. The idea of technocracy is important because it designates an entirely different process. In a society in which politics is the social control of the rationalized economy, it is logical that the rationalizers, the managers of public or private enterprises, revive the ideology of the entrepreneurs and heads of firms, because they identify the interests of the citizens with the power of the economy and the firms. This tendency is reinforced by two principal facts. Mass production is more strongly bound than before to mass consumption, which calls forth the affirmation of unity between rationalization and politics. On the other hand, an increasing proportion of investments are removed from any criterion of bringing in a return. Science and power are more and more closely allied and societies which dispose of a great abundance of goods can dedicate an increasing portion of them to scientific and military research and accomplishments. The staggering growth of "research and development" expenditures in the United States and the Soviet Union and the enormous cost of the nuclear and space industries have broadened the area in which firms can act simply in the name of the progress of knowledge and power.

Is it necessary to recall the responses that this double technocratic pretension arouses? The bond between mass production and consumption does not mean that the progress of production will naturally end in the best possible satisfaction of human needs and in the most rational organization of social life. Needs can be created or reinforced artifically: priority can be given to investments that are less useful than others—to superhighways rather than housing, for example. Even more violent is the contradiction that is set up between the politics of power and the satisfaction of human needs, between stockpiles of nuclear arms and the hunger of the Third World. We recall these well-known and dramatically true responses to the utopias and ambitions of the technocracy only to stress that in this modern type of industrial society, these *programmed societies,* the principles of analysis utilized thus far continue to be applicable.

The technocratic managers defend the power of the production system and oppose it to consumer needs that they combat or deform. The image of society to which they refer themselves is that of ceaselessly growing productivity which brings about in some natural way the amelioration of the social conditions of life. This vision of the world is opposed to that of the workers who no longer define themselves by their craft or skill but by their professional status, their working life, and their career—private principles that occupy a parallel place to that of the power of the firms for the managers.

What the workers oppose is likewise the counterpart of what the managers defend: the permanent transformation of social life in terms of the needs of production—the workers' continuity in their personal existence, the capacity to plan ahead, and to choose their work and their living conditions. The image to which they refer themselves is that of a society of abundance, or rather of liberty, in which surpluses are utilized in terms of needs arranged on the basis of the life experiences of groups and of the activity of voluntary organizations.

In these societies of development, the State cannot remain a particular sphere, separated from civil society. It intervenes in the life of the firm in a great variety of ways. But it is legitimate to consider that, within the general logic of this system of production, the managers, wage-earners, and the State are assuredly independent agents but that their orientations of their activity are connected within a system of action that is not so much increasingly unified as increasingly integrated.

It has appeared useful to define unionism in this situation as a unionism of control.[9] This word indicates the two-fold orientation of unionism. It cannot limit itself to being an agent of demands without concern for economic rationality; neither can it assume economic responsibilities that are never really granted to it and content itself with playing a role of social integration: the fusion of direct social responsibility with indirect economic responsibility. Firms, that is, their managers, have everywhere been led to be concerned with general social problems that touch social organization of the communities in which they are located (educational programs and the extension of education) foreseeing and dealing with the consequences of technical changes, as well as with geographic transfers of economic activity, etc.

Just as the unions' control of economic activity demands their penetration into the firm, so the managers' control of social organization presses them to emerge from the firm and to become social leaders. But these two movements remain necessarily limited and the idea of a management of firms by the workers, isolated from the overriding objective of over-all political transformation, seems as anachronistic as that of the management of society by the industrial managers. It is the State's role to insure the greatest possible communication between the firm and society. This is why Harbison and Myers were right to consider that constitutional management is the

[9] Alain Touraine, "Le Syndicalisme de controle," *Cahiers internationaux de sociologie* (Jan.–June 1960) : 57–88.

most characteristic form of management for modern firms. This penetration of the State into the social relationships of work is the counterpart of the penetration of economic leaders and the labor unions into the elaboration or control of the economic policies of the State.

These observations do not at all aim at demonstrating that the firm, conceived as a private institution, reaches a greater and greater degree of balance or harmony. This hypothesis has as little foundation as those that affirm the absolute power of the State over the whole of economic life, the omnipotence of economic leaders, or the possibility of a management of the economy by working communities. While we can speak of the institutional reinforcement of the firm, this has a quite different meaning. To the degree that rationalizing models spread in economic life, the involved parties are more and more defined by their relations and by the system of social governance of economic rationality that these relations constitute. This intervention makes each of the involved parties even more vulnerable by forbidding it to enclose itself within its own sphere. It also forces analysis to reverse traditional classifications. Is it still possible to propose independent sociological analysis of the working class, the owners, or the State when each of these is defined more and more by its role within a political system whose unity comes not from domination by one of them—even if this is strongly marked—but from its main problem, the social utilization of economic rationality?

Do not this unity and its political nature force it to be located uniquely on the societal level, that of the principal political institutions? We will not be able to answer this question until the last part of this study, but for now we must say that one of the fundamental traits of programmed societies is the weakening of the traditional identity between the political system and the State. The worker-consumer is more and more led to combat technocratic and Statist pretensions by reinforcing community organizations, whether regional, local, or professional, because only by concrete social and cultural membership in them can the individual be defended. Everywhere we see the new importance of "ascribed status," of what man is as opposed to what he does. Likewise, the firm is a particular phenomenon, the depository of limited rationalizing models, in the name of which it struggles both against Statism and against the risks of immobilism on the part of the community-oriented movements. The State, firms, and the community groups interact within the political system because the principles of defense, opposition, and totality that constitute each of their systematic orientations mix in an increasingly complex and integrated way.

This analysis of the most modern type of firm leads to complex conclusions, for one can interpret it in two quite different, almost opposed manners. On one side, the firm increasingly appears as a political institution, both as a center of decision-making and programming and a center of social negotiations dealing with relations between techno-economic progress and the improvement of the living and working conditions of wage-earners. On the other hand, it seems subordinated to a higher system of decision-making on the level of the State. This level possesses more and more important instruments of economic action which it commits, itself, to activities less and less governed by criteria of economic return. The firm then becomes merely an instrument, an organization whose independence of decision indicates the necessary decentralization of a complex economic system.

This same ambiguity comes up again when we seek to define the role of unions. On one side, with the leaders of the Italian C.G.I.L.* like Trentin or with certain French union leaders, especially in the C.F.D.T.,† one can insist on the penetration of union action into the level of the policy decisions of the firm; on the other hand, one can think that unions negotiate more and more the conditions of work, employment, and promotion, while becoming less and less the leaders of new social struggles. These struggles are directed more against the politico-economic power of the State, bound to the great financial and industrial groups. They are in active defense of community groups, defined less by work than by their resistance to economic, social, and cultural change, over which they exercise no control and which therefore appears to them as a force of alienation.

We will see further on that these two aspects of the firm are combined in different ways according to the type of society under consideration. But their close relationship should lead us from now on to a reexamination of the notion of institution as we have used it up to this point. The firm is an institution insofar as it is more than an organization but less than a power. It is the place where social forces negotiate and arrive at a definition of the rules and forms of their confrontation, that is, the institutionalization of their conflict. On the level of the organization, collective relations of work aim at insuring the cohesiveness of the whole, the diminution of relative

---

* Confederazione Generale Italiano del Lavoro, the largest communist-led Italian trade union.

† Confederation Française et Démocratique du Travail. Formerly C.F.T.C. (Christian workers' union), it dropped in 1964 all references to Church's social teaching and was instrumental in introducing new types of grievances.

privation, the attenuation of inequalities, the reinforcement of statuses that fit together. On the level of power,
on the contrary, more or less established and self-conscious
social classes oppose each other by striving to dominate
the whole process of economic and social change. Each of
the adversaries identifies itself in a utopian way with the
general interest and ideologically opposes the opposite
camp.

Institutionalization is halfway between these two levels
of social relations. Social forces in negotiation do not define themselves relative to society as a whole but in relation to the particular and limited framework of the firm;
neither, however, do they place themselves on the level of
the organization, the division of labor, the system of status
and role. It would be dangerous to set up a simple opposition between the political strength and the organizational strength of the firm; dangerous also to believe that
unionism is split between directly political action and
strictly professional and economic intervention, limited
to the internal problems of the firm. Economic efforts and
social relations are organized on an intermediary level in
very diverse forms.

The firm is increasingly situated on the level of institution. It possesses an independent system for economic
decision-making and social negotiation. At the same time,
it is an element within a power system (hence a system
of social conflicts that largely transcend it) because economic progress is only vaguely determined by the accumulation of capital and the organization of labor, and
increasingly by scientific and technical research, professional training and retraining, the mobility of information
and production factors, the capacity for planning activity,
etc.

The great social conflicts transcend the firm and the whole area of production and are situated, like programmed change itself, on a much broader plane. They are multidimensional—social, cultural, and political—much more than strictly economic. The distinction between these two roles of the firm is most often indicated by the use of the word *political.* This word has two meanings: the exercise of power and a system of decision-making. One can speak of a system of decision-making to the degree that a concrete agent—individual or collective—seeks to attain certain objectives that it believes conform to its own interests; it seeks to do so by entering into interaction with other agents, who may be allied, parallel, or hostile. Power, on the contrary, is defined by the capacity of certain agents to impose on all the other agents their own conception of society, its objectives, and its manner of evolution. Power defines the field of social action: decision is a process of interaction within this field.

Power and decision-making are never either entirely separated nor entirely confused. The capacity for decision-making is defined by influence, that is, the possibility for a particular agent to modify the behavior of another without himself undergoing comparable modifications of his own behavior. Management and unions negotiate and seek to modify each other's behavior. The system of decision-making can be more or less institutionalized within the political systems of the firm.

But the economic leaders also exercise domination, a social control that comes into conflict with an opposed model of direction and social change defended by their adversaries. To the degree that economic progress supposes a broader intervention of society within its own development, the problems of power increasingly tran-

scend the firm. This is what allows a certain institutionalization of industrial conflict and the creation of political
institutions within the firm that deal with problems that
go far beyond the internal management of an organization of work.

In an earlier stage of the firm, there does not seem to
have been an intermediary between the problems of power
and those of professional life, largely regulated within
independent professional working groups. Industrial evolution leads to a growing differentiation among the
working levels of the firm and particularly to the strengthening of the institutional level midway between the
problems of power and those that relate to the internal
functioning of organizations. We must now focus on this
differentiation.

## Differentiation of the Levels of Functioning

Analytically, strengthening of the firm as an institution
follows the progress of its organization. How is the role of
the manager bound to that of the organizer; how is the
policy of the firm bound to its functioning? At the beginning we said—and everything that has just been said is
a commentary on this general idea—that the firm is not
only an organization; it is also a decision-making system,
that in its turn, within the sphere of execution and organization, rationalizes itself at the same time that it
politicizes itself. Therefore, a return to the conceptions of
the head of the firm as a simple organizer or coordinator
of material and human means of production is excluded.
But, having recognized the importance of the firm as an
institution, we must go further back and inquire into the

relations between these two levels of the working of the firm.

At first, one may be tempted to think that one of the principal aspects of the revolution that has just been recalled is the increasingly direct domination exercised by one level of functioning over one or both below it: has not the organization of work suppressed, or at least greatly diminished, the professional independence of manufacturing workers as well as the direct dependence of the firm on the market? Likewise, is it not logical to think that the sphere of organization tends to be more and more subject to that of decision-making, the politics of the firm? The problems of execution have not simply been absorbed by those of organization; to a certain degree, they have been institutionalized due to the influence of the unions and to social laws. Is it not even more true that the problems posed by the organization of firms are more and more carried up to the institutional level and that the unions carry out within the firm a social policy that includes the problems posed both by execution as well as by the organization of work?

The reality and importance of this development are hardly arguable. Neither the firm nor the union can isolate from more general problems the demands that touch on working conditions, the setting of qualifications, professional training and promotion, work schedules and hours. Above all, the amount and forms of remuneration are more and more directly bound to the general functioning of the firm and the economy. Tied at first to production or skills, it was later tied to output and finally to productivity. Today, it is never separated from the more general problems of economic policy: the parallelism between economic growth and raising living standards, policy concerning revenues, inflation, etc.

These observations are so easy to grasp that they scarcely cast any light on the problem we have posed. In particular, it is evident that the problems of remuneration always arose from the firm's policies and not from its system of execution, even when the bases on which it was calculated were on that level. It is natural that the growing institutionalization of the firm should bring about a parallel transformation of both worker demands and of the formation of the heads of the firm. But does this mean that the problems of organization tend to be resolved in those of the institutional working of the firm? Certainly not. This statement is equally applicable to the autonomy of the problems of the execution of work properly so-called.

The increasing politicalization of the firm does not diminish but actually accentuates its organizational constraints. The thesis according to which the organizational problems are reabsorbed into the "institutional" problems of the firm can be formulated in the following way: the management of the firm increasingly consists in combining the more and more complex strategies of more and more numerous agents whose capacity to exert influence is likewise increasing. This conception has the very great merit of avoiding once and for all an image borrowed from a much earlier state of organizations which has been spread in sociological thought because of Weber's concept of bureaucracy.

The army, the public administration, and later the great firms sought for a long period to define the functions, rights, and duties of their members. The construction of organizational charts was the most concrete expression of such an effort. But many sociologists like Peter Blau, Tom Burns, and Michel Crozier demonstrated that an organization subject to frequent changes could not function in this manner. The dysfunctions of this bureaucratic management are such that it has been replaced by an entirely different kind of organization. It is no longer the rule that governs, but the objective. It is no longer the service or the department, but this particular program that establishes the fundamental unity of action. Public opinion has long since grown used to this change in vocabulary, at least since the success of such massive operations as the invasion landings of 1944.

We have come to consider the firm as a strategic field whose management primarily performs the task of negotiation. The firm's adaptation to change will improve to the degree that it is more pragmatic, less burdened with principles and rules, more careful to insure among its various elements an adaptation that is always limited and provisional. The mechanistic conception of the firm has been replaced by the image of a market dealing in influences, a market whose balance is unstable and consequently more favorable to change and to adaptation to an environment that is itself changing. Crozier expressed this conception very precisely when he emphasized that the more modern an organization was, the more it would include "zones of uncertitude" which the various participants would strive to control in order to strengthen their influence within the organization.

These analyses have great importance and render the discussions on the bureaucratic model defined by Weber almost without interest; they must be considered only as an archaic form of organization. But these analyses must nevertheless be completed. A firm is not exclusively a market dealing in influence and a place where autonomous strategies confront or combine with each other; it is also an organization that possesses a center of decision-making and boundaries, and imposes on its members a "loyalty" that allows the strategies to maintain themselves within quite narrow limits. The very flexibility of the styles of organization imposes more and more potent mechanisms of social integration.

When the system of rules and norms is clear and stable, it is not necessary to interfere with attitudes and intentions. Everyone is placed in a box of the organizational chart. He knows what is forbidden and what is demanded. To the degree that the objective limits disappear, it becomes necessary that all the members of the organization be oriented toward its integration, that they interiorize its values and norms and acquire a "house spirit." One must certainly distrust the whole literature—of which William H. Whyte, Jr.'s *The Organization Man* is the best known example—that presents the lower ranking executives in particular as dominated by "status anxiety." But to insist too exclusively on the possibilities of the autonomous strategies of the greatest number would be to fall into an opposite exaggeration. For influence increases with hierarchical authority and strategy consists in rising and hence in identifying oneself with the official values of the organization. In the most modern and most technical organizations, marked by the increasing interdependence of functions and the presence of strong values, science and health combine their efforts to increase the pressure from forces of social integration, the recognition of values, norms, hierarchies, and social conduct proper to the organization.

To the same degree that the fundamental mechanics of

economic progress are no longer determined on the level of the firm itself (as used to be the case during the period of entrepreneurial capitalism) but on a higher level, so the firm becomes an organization that is pragmatic in its aims and highly integrative. It becomes less an assemblage of working assignments and specialities and more of a communications network whose unity can be maintained only through pressure to conform to the needs of the organization, its homogeneity, and its capacity to avoid change and incidents. One consequence of this is the growing importance of the problems dealt with by mixed worker-management committees, instruments less of negotiation than of integration. Another consequence is the firm's very manifest concern for information and an equal concern over careers and promotion.

The problems of the organization are separated from those that relate to institutionalized negotiations and, *a fortiori*, from the problems of power. As a result, relations among the various working levels in the firm are complex. Institutionalization gets beyond the organization to the degree that the firm becomes more and more of a political unit. The internal problems of the organization resist the institutionalization of decisions and conflicts which is necessarily limited and also because the strength of the firm lies in its organization. Authority is not reduced to more influence but is primarily the organizational expression of power.

This leads us to two complementary themes. On the one hand, the firm is increasingly a systematization of political decisions and negotiations identified neither with its organization system nor its system power. On the other hand, the functional problems of the organizations have greater and greater autonomy based on the power of the owners.

In other words, if one directly considers these problems, one sees that they simultaneously lend themselves to three types of analysis. First, certain aspects of the social relations of work refer to a purely organizational study: a firm has norms and rules; it defines roles and styles of interaction; it is differentiated and hierarchized. Secondly, its institutional system penetrates the sphere of organization, especially to the degree that the unions can once again professionally and economically defend the wage-earners within the framework of a broader strategy. Finally, the cultural trends and power conflicts of society at large are also at work within the firm and define its values and norms.

This differentiation of three levels of analysis does not mean to imply the existence of three separate sets of social facts. Rather it relates different problems and their various meanings. Analysis of the firm simply as a system of institutional decisions and negotiations would neglect both its mechanisms of social integration and its power problems. On the other hand, exclusive insistence on the direct link between organizational functioning and the system of power would ignore the element that explains the economic and social autonomy of the firm.

When analysis grants the insufficiency of purely psycho-sociological study of the firm, and correctly brings up the problems involved in decision-making and power, there is fruitful tension between the two approaches we have distinguished. Institutional analysis must be balanced by an analysis that insists on the reality of power expressed both directly and through organizational problems.

This represents a reversal of perspectives in terms of older analyses that corresponded to the first stages of the evolution we have traced. They insisted on the extremes:

economic power and professional autonomy face to face. On the contrary, one must place institutional realities, systems of decision, and negotiation at the center of the picture. But one also must constantly present the allied and contrary pressures exercised over them both by the functioning of the organization and by power conflicts.

It is more difficult to speak of an increasing autonomy for the problems of technical execution, since the most obvious trait of industrial evolution is that the organizational system exercises more and more control over the way in which execution is carried out and, even more so, because the professional autonomy of the manufacturing worker has largely disappeared. But we do not need to return to such observations. The evolution of the system of production does not entail the disappearance of the social problems and social behavior directly located at the job level. Quite the contrary; on all levels of the organization, the diversity of jobs and specialities poses increasingly complex problems. They are clearest in terms of staff personnel, where we note the progress of professionalization and the growing importance of occupational behavior as reflected in levels of authority. Many of the observations made by sociologists of organizations clearly demonstrate the importance of the experts and, as a result, the possibilities open to them for maneuvers and strategy within the organization. But this is no longer a matter of institutionalized negotiations or relationships among social forces. It is a matter of personal strategies that may form coalitions but still aim at bettering the positions of the concerned individuals within—or, better, in the face of—the organizational system.

We must go further. Social evolution, the raising of living standards, the too slow increase in free time, the development of leisure activities, and the importance of family life as a center of consumption and interpersonal relations contribute to the creation of professional behavior determinants that are increasingly independent of the firm. Goldthorpe, Lockwood, and their collaborators [10] strongly emphasized this point in their study of economically privileged English workers in very modern situations. The workers define themselves less and less in terms of their professional activity. Their roles outside the firm —bound to family, neighborhood, habits of consumption —are increasingly important to them. This necessarily means that occupational behavior, the choice of a job, attitudes toward remuneration, and interest in work, etc. are all determined from outside. Work is a means to consumption.

At the top of the production system, we see that the centers of decision move out of the firm and rise to the level of the State and the massive national or international economic groups. In a parallel way, at its base we see the traditional image of the worker disappear. In particular, managers—at least when they are young—tend more and more to seek a place of employment that favors their children's education and their own leisure. The firm used to be the center of the economic and social organization; the worker's life was directly and indirectly dominated by it. Economic life was almost nothing more than the interaction between firms and the market.

Today, society invades the firm through two routes so that one is led to define it now as the association of an institutional system with an organizational system. This

[10] J. H. Goldthorpe, D. Lockwood, F. Bachofer, and J. Platt, *The Affluent Worker: Industrial Attitudes and Behavior,* vol. I (Cambridge University Press, 1968).

double-faced economic unit is located between the economic powers and the employee's private life. The strengthening of the organization and its mechanisms of social integration often comes into conflict with the development of negotiations, the institutionalization of conflicts. These two processes develop concurrently, for both represent centripetal tendencies of a firm threatened by centrifugal forces both at its summit and its base. We must recognize that such a weakening of the firm necessarily brings about a limitation of the social importance of labor unionism, insofar as it is still defined by its relationship with its adversary, management. It mobilizes a diminishing part of the personality; it is also further from the fundamental political conflicts of society. The activity of union leaders, their active participation in both political activities and community associations outside of work, witnesses their militancy but does not contradict—and may even corroborate—the shrinking area in which the unions act.

It is necessary to ask if this shrinking, the weakening of the passions aroused by unions, does not make the militant and democratic participation of the workers in the decisions and workings of their union more difficult. The most militant elements focus either on political commitment or on cultural demands and social revolt that largely transcend the framework of the firm. Within the firm, it is a matter of defense, management, integration of the organizational system, and, above all, more and more institutionalized negotiations. Union leaders are not integrated into the government of the firm; most often they retain a very combative spirit, but this is not the same thing as militancy. The evolution and essential choices of society are less and less the focus of their action.

In the case of France, the authoritarianism of the owners
and the State, the multiple resistances to the institutionalization of conflicts, the attachment to archaic styles of
management and forms of authority, the nature of the
political system, all contribute to keeping both firms and
unions locked into forms of action that seem very far from
the image we have just outlined. These delays and the
slow evolution must not hide the direction being taken
there as well as elsewhere. Our economic and social past
was dominated by the central confrontation between the
firm and the company-oriented union.* Today, the two
adversaries continue to oppose each other but their combat
no longer involves all the levels of social life but is situated on intermediary levels—which still leaves it considerable importance. It exerts less direct and complete
influence than before on the economic and social politics
of society and the private lives of the workers.

The world of the entrepreneur and the labor militant
still exists but it is increasingly subordinated to the centers
of programming and of cultural revolts. This does not at
all mean that union leaders can intervene only on the
institutional and organizational levels. But if unionism
within the firm, which has often appeared as an objective
of militant action, indicates real progress in terms of
union interference with the authoritarianism of the owners, it is important on the organizational and institutional
levels only because it is thereby removed from the struggle
over economic and political power.

As a result, unionism no longer tends to be the central

* In the French, *syndicalisme d'entreprise*. It is a catchword for union
leadership that wanted militant action directed at the internal problems
of a company, rather than to more general political problems. Such action
cannot be considered an attack against the economic order.

instrument of a social movement that transcends it both at its summit and base, that is, on the specifically political level and on the level of resistance to the organizational integration and institutionalization of social conflicts. At the same time that unionism gains influence and intervenes more effectively on the level of decisions, it is ignored, bypassed, or opposed by the antitechnocratic movements that are both more political and less well organized.

These conclusions go a little beyond what we set out to discuss. But they outline the general framework into which this increasing differentiation among the levels of functioning of the production system must be placed.

## The Diversity Among Industrial Societies

Relations among the different functioning levels of the firm depend primarily on the kind of economic development that characterizes the society as a whole. The more the work of economic development is directed by an explicit social intention, or the more bound it is to a social and political movement, whether of national independence or social change, the less will the tension between economic development and social democracy be institutionalized and the more powerfully will the policy level of the firm control its organizational and institutional levels. On the contrary, a more "open" society, less committed to a voluntary effort to emerge from dependence or underdevelopment and to break down cultural, institutional, and political resistance to economic development, is more "pluralist": the objectives of development will not be determined by a central political power but will be worked out through institutionalized negotiations. At the same time, the autonomy of the working levels of the firm will tend to outweigh their hierarchization.

This opposition, which may seem satisfactory at first sight, must be completed by another proposition, because it supposes a complete parallelism between the firm and the national economy. If one were satisfied with that, one would have to deny the essential element of our analysis, the idea that every modern industrial system is defined both by the control of the political system over the working levels of the firm and also by the relative autonomy of the different systems.

We must then correct the overly simple formulation that has just been given and inquire how, in a liberal type of economic growth, the control exercised by a weak political will on the national level can still be asserted on the level of the firm. In the opposite way, in a more managed type of economic growth, where economic activity is directed by "active power," in Bertrand de Jouvenel's expression, the relative autonomy of the working levels in the firm perhaps tends to be reinforced and thus to compensate for the integrative and unifying tendency operative on the national level.

a). We will call the first type of industrial society *liberal*. Its three principal characteristics are strong integration of the social relations of work, very advanced development of the constitutional management of firms, and weak penetration of rationalizing models on the level of decision-making. The private interests of firms remain powerful for the simple reason that the idea of development is only weakly "politicized" and political power interferes very little with the firm.

The risk inherent in this type is the reduction of the political level of the firm to its institutional level. The power of the unions to intervene and the role of the State are combined to increase the importance of and improve the treatment of the internal social problems of the firm. The head of the firm is often a coordinator. But only in pathological situations is the idea of development forgotten. Most often, especially in dynamic firms, it is present— but abstractly, that is, without being recognized as the focus of social struggles. It is defined as social change, as the capacity of the firm to adapt itself to new conditions by overcoming its own rigidities. Development is defined as continuing modernization assured by the triumph of rational calculations over traditions and ideologies opposed to effective adaptation to the present. In liberal societies, ends are abstract and means concrete; the accent is on the rationality of the means. But it is impossible for this tendency to dominate completely. The absence of political direction over development has for its normal corollary the reinforcement of the massive firm as a political unit. Not only is it the place where great economic decisions are made but it also tends to reinforce its social integration and hence to reduce the autonomy of the subsystems of technical execution and organization relative to its private political system.

The firm tends to define itself as a tool of social integration. It controls and organizes economic expectations, careers, social relations, and sometimes activities outside of work. It is not a pure system of decision-making and negotiation. Within it, power, institution, and organization are meshed, an integration that makes the firm the pivot of economic and social life. The most liberal economy is dominated by the massive corporations. One can perhaps go so far as to say that when a firm of this type is deliberately oriented toward development, the constitutional nature of its management tends to become attenuated. It is striking to note that Harbison and Myers, for example, number such modern firms as Kodak and IBM among the paternalistic firms in the United States. Durand [11] has made similar observations in France. One especially thinks, in this regard, of the great firms of German heavy industry, whose authoritarianism Hartmann [12] has described, or of the Japanese firms described by James C. Abegglen.[13]

In liberal societies, union activity has little influence in the area of economic policy. On the other hand, it contributes greatly to the development in firms of a private legal system resting on very elaborate collective agreements, crowned in the United States especially by an extremely effective grievance procedure that assures the good social functioning of the firm conceived as an organization. The essential contribution of union activity is kept within the firm to the degree that the firm is economically autonomous and its decision-making system only slightly subject to societal politics.

b) . *Planned or voluntarist societies* are characterized by three complementary traits. In the first place, the relations and tensions between the central objective of economic development and the social forces that aim at controlling it are very weakly institutionalized. In an extreme situation, complete identification of political intention and economic activity is imposed by authority defined by the struggle against dependence or archaism. In the second place, the political decision-making system of the firm has

[11] C. Durand, "La signification des politiques de formation et de promotion," *Sociologie du travail* (Oct.–Dec., 1963) : 316–328.

[12] H. Hartmann, *Authority and Organization in German Management* (Princeton University Press, 1959) .

[13] James C. Abegglen, *The Japanese Factory: Aspects of its Social Organization* (Glencoe, Ill.: Free Press, 1958) .

very little autonomy. The firm is a production unit whose objectives and means of action are determined by political power. Finally, and this is less evident, the consequence of the two preceding observations is that within the firm the organization and technical execution subsystems have great independence: the firm's capacity for political integration is weak.

In this situation, the internal problems of social administration have the greatest autonomy. The several studies available to us of firms in Soviet-type countries show the extreme importance of the role of the unions in setting working and employment conditions. This explains in particular why it is so difficult to translate technical changes into modifications of the labor force. Often, workers are too numerous for a given production.

At the same time, the wage-earners define their interests and objectives in very individual terms, which frequently causes great resistance from the informal organization whose norms are sometimes openly opposed to those of the firm. The most voluntarist systems are also the ones most exposed to strong bureaucratization in the current sense of this term. In other words, they are exposed to a strong autonomy on the part of the systems of means relative to the objectives of the firm. The Yugoslav policy of self-management is an important effort aimed at recognizing and organizing this bipolarity and establishing at the base of firms, on the level of individual plants, a capacity for decision-making opposed to the centralizing influences of an economic organization that is dominated by the communists' league. Its success places the management of firms in a difficult situation. This is why the managers strive to play on their political involvement to oppose pressure from the base and on the interests of their firms to cut down on control by central authority.

It must be added that this bureaucratization reaches its most pronounced forms in a situation that combines certain aspects of the two extreme types we have distinguished, that is, when concentration of decision-making power on the level of the State is combined with a strong institutionalization of social conflicts. The power of economic leadership risks being absorbed by defensive social policies, while the capacity for economic decision-making on the level of the firm remains weak. This situation is often observed in societies that are marked more by economic management than by economic planning. If we consider public education as an economic activity, we can see in the French university system of recent years an extreme case of the degeneration of the voluntarist type. Objectives of development have been largely subjected to corporate interests. At the same time, individual units of production have no power to make decisions. The result is extreme autonomy in terms of execution and organization and a strange union between bureaucratization and liberalism, centralization and local liberties.

The management of firms in a voluntarist type of society labors under extreme weakness. Its capacity for initiative is limited both by decisions made on a higher level and by the organization's resistance to its decisions. It is forced to strengthen its formal authority, to develop whatever can protect it against what is above and below it, to multiply rules and prohibitions, and to increase the distances between the hierarchical levels in order to escape the pressures that weigh on it. When it has the opportunity, it fights for the decentralization of decision-making and for the autonomy of the management units.

c) . It is possible to distinguish many intermediate types

between these two extremes. We shall be content to designate them by the general term of *contractual societies*. Such societies are simultaneously voluntarist and liberal; they consciously refer to rationalizing models at the same time as they strongly institutionalize the general social conflicts. They constantly run the risk that these two directions will cancel each other out. Firms may think of themselves as public services in which the unions can exercise such power as to greatly limit management's freedom to make decisions. The managers in this case are stripped of economic freedom because it is either pushed upward to organs of the State or reduced to a rigid emphasis on technique. The social failure of certain nationalized French firms illustrates this. On the other hand, the system may be balanced by the admission that economic and social policy (while joined on the level of the firm) each enjoy a certain autonomy. This is achieved, for example, in Swedish society where the unions have government support and the heads of firms remain tied to properly capitalist power. The opposite case can likewise be considered, where the managers are supported by the political power and the unions have great social influence and important access to power within the firm. This image seems to correspond to the reform of the firm proposed by F. Bloch-Lainé.[14] In his scheme, union participation would move beyond the level of the organization and penetrate into the decision-making system; but the autonomy of the manager is maintained.

The Swedish version of the contractual society is closer to a liberal society; the version proposed by F. Bloch-Lainé is closer to a voluntarist model. The first gives an

[14] F. Bloch-Lainé, *Pour une reforme de l'entreprise* (Paris: Editions du Seuil, 1963).

essential role to public institutions, while the second insists especially on the contractual relations between employers and employees. The role assigned to the State in
France is characteristic less of the traditions of the country
than of the difficulties of establishing directly contractual
relations because of both authoritarianism of the owners
and the revolutionary ideology of the C.G.T.* The important thing here is not to measure what chances either
type has to succeed, but to recognize that the nature of a
contractual society supposes both strong political influence
on the part of the unions and the maintenance of the firm
as a private institution.

The role of the union in the firm varies very much
among the types of industrial societies. In liberal societies,
it is appropriate to say that unions' objectives are mostly
within the company itself since the power of economic
decision-making remains private and the intervention of
the unions is on the level of organization and institution,
either directly or by means of mixed or representative
consultative bodies. In managed or voluntarist societies,
the union's action is necessarily primarily political. Unionism is strongly centralized and strives to intervene in
economic policy both by direct pressure and by participation in those bodies in which economic decisions are
worked out. At the same time, it exercises powerful defensive action at the base, while in a liberal system the
union's action in the firm does not separate economic
demands from participation in the organisms that inte-
grate the social system of the firm.

In each of the two cases, unionism is caught between
opposed exigencies. In one case, it is associated with polit-

* Conféderation générale du travail, the largest communist-oriented
trade union in France.

ical power while in the firm it is almost fused with the informal organizations; in the other case, it primarily acts on the level of the firm but is simultaneously, on this intermediate level, an instrument of economic opposition to management and a means of social integration. Finally, in contractual societies, union action is most often on an intermediate level of industrial federations or branches of industry.

The interest manifested in France today in favor of the legal recognition of the local union (*section syndicale*) of the firm is far from clear. It arises from an unarguable fact: the private French firm remains essentially dominated by an autocratic or paternalistic style of management. But beyond this realization, approaches vary. Some think primarily of adapting unionism to a neo-liberal situation, obtaining for it the right to intervene in the social organization of the firm, the result of which would mean acceptance of a private system of decision-making. Others would reinforce the union's power to negotiate by the development of collective agreements. Finally, still others seek to obtain for the union, beyond the firm, some important access to the power of economic decision-making; this is often called democratic planning.

## Final Remarks

This diversity forbids us to have recourse to certain ideas in current use, like the idea of industrial democracy. One could have recourse to this, if one takes the stand for what we have called contractual societies. Does not "industrial democracy" defend a type of labor relations that goes beyond salary grievances but falls short of socialist action directed toward the taking of power? It can include such diverse experiences, fortunate and unfortunate, as the Weimar Republic, Swedish democratic society, and the English Labour Party. Used in this way, this idea is an object for study and suggests an ideology more than a particular problem. But it is dangerous because it mixes aspects of the social problems of the firm with those of economic life.

I wished to show, on the contrary, that these problems are relatively autonomous according to whether they are posed on the level of execution, organization, decision-making, or power. More broadly, the firm is not a "society" and neither is it a simple element of a political system. It exists only because it is a particular unit of decision-making (whether public or private), but it is a firm—and not only an organization—only to the degree that the social conflicts that orient society as a whole are manifested within it.

Our analysis insists especially on the firm defined as an institution; this notion must be further developed. The firm is not only an institution; it participates in the system of economic power and consequently interprets the cultural directions of a society in terms of the interests of the dominant class. The firm has power and seeks to impose both within and outside itself social and cultural conduct matching its class interests. At the same time, the firm is not simply a central element of the system of social production and domination. It is a particular economic, social, and professional unit. It is, consequently, an organization and, even more simply, a place of work. This particularity explains why a union can never be a purely political association, since it must be preoccupied with economic demands within the framework both of the existing power system and of the problems posed by the functioning of an organization.

The firm possesses an autonomous institutional system to the degree that it insures passage from the level of power to the level of organization. These are actually two main hinges: the shop stewards, the foremen, and what American practice calls grievance procedures. The first one links the institutional system to the power system. It is represented by upper-level executives and by unions' political action. The other one links the institutional with the organizational system. It is operated by first-line supervisors and shop stewards who deal with the grievance procedures.

Consequently, the firm is an institution because it is an economic unity as well as the ground for relatively autonomous social negotiations relative to the cultural orientations and class conflicts of society as a whole—autonomous, not independent. The power of the head of the firm is assuredly inseparable from the type of production or from the nature of the dominant class; and union action cannot be isolated from the worker movement that is also expressed in the class conflict. The central importance of these connections rules out considering the firm merely as an organization.

The institutional level must not be confused with that of the cultural orientations and general struggles of society any more than with the level of organization. This level exists only because we consider the firm as a concrete whole, whose decisions are not pure social and cultural orientations but also means to defend the interests of one particular unit against other interests and under conditions of action defined in time and space. Likewise, one can speak of a political institution only when one consid-

ers, not a society, but a State and a nation limited by
boundaries and possessing a center of decision-making.

Within this concrete framework there exist organized
social forces whose nature and interests do not directly express the classes that are in conflict; neither do they simply
correspond to the interests of status groups defined by
their place in the organization. These social forces can
institutionalize their relations only to the degree that they
agree to define themselves in terms of the firm, its limits
and particular characteristics. The complexity of professional relations in industry results from the fact that they
must always combine negotiations within a given framework with opposed class interests which constantly transcend the limited framework of the firm.

The firm has an economic function, generally accepted by those who work in it. But there is debate about
the control and social utilization of production. In this
sense, the firm is an institution only when it recognizes
these conflicts and the organizations which defend the
interests of the involved parties, particularly the unions.
If the firm were only an organization, it could certainly be
a place of strategies and negotiations but the involved
parties would work only to improve their relative positions in the social system of the firm. The firm is institutionalized because it is an element of a real society
in which the problems of power are posed. On the other
hand, if the firm had no autonomy in society, it would
suffice to apply to it laws and decisions made on the level
of the State.

The firm is neither a political entity nor just a simple
instrumental organization. Its dependence on the social
power gives its institutional mechanisms their center of
reference; its particularity obliges specific agents to

negotiate their relations within the framework of a unit of production and a system of decision-making. The evolution of the firm reinforces the institutionalization of the social relations that are formed there, since it increasingly differentiates the level of economic policy from that of the organization or internal management at the same time as it makes them increasingly interdependent.

These general considerations have practical consequences and cast light on problems that are usually posed in different terms. The evolution of the firm leads the unions neither to increasingly political action nor to intervention limited to the internal problems of the organization. It gives them an increasingly important institutional role, located halfway between the political and the organizational spheres.

The unions intervene more and more in the sphere of economic policy. But if they involve themselves there completely, either to tie themselves to the State or to fight it directly, they are no more than a political group and lose all possibility of intervening in the internal problems of the firm; consequently, they lose their proper base. They are condemned to be only the industrial cell of the party. On the other hand, unionism that limits itself to professional and organizational problems risks growing weak and becoming an instrument of social integration and promotion by cutting itself off from the forces of political and social contestation. This second situation is met more commonly in liberal societies, while the first is more common in voluntarist societies. This is why unionism has the greatest importance in contractual societies and why in such societies it is most constantly caught between necessarily opposed exigencies. It is always both in opposition and party to negotiation, reformist and revolutionary.

One can present the situation of management in analogous terms. In liberal societies more than others, it is an element of the power system; in voluntarist societies, it is primarily the direction of an organization. In contractual societies, it has a double role as economic power and social negotiator. At the beginning of the evolution that we have sketched, such problems did not exist. The action of both the union and the owner was situated more simply on the level of economic power and the labor market. The internal problems of the firm were directly related to the economic system and the confrontation between interests. Political forces appeared primarily as instruments—more or less well adapted—at the service of social interests whose conflict directly dominated the firm. Today, on the contrary, the increasing autonomy of the problems of organization and of institutionalized negotiations gives the conflicts within the firm both a general political significance and a certain autonomy.

This is why neither the head of the firm nor the union organization is the central protagonist of social and political conflicts. This is the meaning of the classic expression *the institutionalization of labor conflicts,* an expression that must be understood correctly. It does not at all mean that these conflicts disappear or are even pacified; neither does it mean that they are depoliticized. It only means that they are particularized at the same time that organizational problems acquire certain political significance.

The interdependence of the levels of functioning in the firm raises the level of demands and allows the unions to connect economic defense more closely to political objectives; but the transformation of the economic system and the conditions of growth lowers the firm's level of action and places it midway between the political and the organizational. This leads us to think that the head of the firm is no longer the central personage of the economic power system and that unionism is no longer the principal instrument of movements for social change.

This conclusion will satisfy neither those for whom the institutionalization of conflicts signifies the return to industrial peace nor those who hope that unionism will more and more directly attack economic power. It indicates the increasing importance of both the unions and the firm in the social organization. It also affirms that in today's programmed society, dominated by the new conflict between technocrats and consumers—for lack of a better term—the confrontation between firm managers and unions is no longer at the center of political struggles.

# IV

†††††††††††††

# Leisure Activities, Social Participation, and Cultural Innovation

*The Decline of Traditional Leisure Activities*

If leisure activities are defined as activities other than work, one would have to include under the term most of the cultural acts of a society—religious life, games, political activity, and sports. Everyone rejects this definition without clearly defining why. The reasons will become clearer if we recall that the theme of leisure activity is almost always associated in the minds of sociologists with the subject of mass society. This is either because they are describing the subjection of individuals to the modern means of communication—mass media—or because they observe the effects of modern work, piecework, which is narrowly defined and performed within massive firms that are governed in such a way that the individual feels that he is connected with them only in terms of his function. These two themes are often connected with each other somewhat this way: the mechanization of work prepares the way for mechanized leisure, and leaves us helpless before the repeated onslaughts of propaganda (understood in the broadest sense).

Without discussing here the value or limitations of this analysis, we retain its general outlines: the question of leisure activities arises as soon as the members of a society come under cultural influences that are no longer connected with the organized activities of a concrete socioeconomic group. As a result, these cultural experiences are no longer understandable on the basis of the individual's professional and social experience.

One hesitates to compare the mass leisure activities of industrial and urban civilization with the folklore or cultural life of rural civilizations and non-industrialized societies. In the latter, the content of the leisure activity is connected with professional and social life. Sometimes the activities are connected quite simply, as in seasonal holidays or celebrations connected with one's work, etc; sometimes in an indirect manner, as when certain free-time activities are intended to compensate for unremitting labor or misery. This bond is almost always accompanied by another that unites free-time activities to the whole social life of the collectivity and usually has geographic reasons: a village feast reunites the inhabitants of a particular village, members of a concrete community. A festival in mining country may be an outlet for needs that are repressed by the work and the life in the mining villages; in any case it is profoundly integrated into the life of a working community.

This two-fold rooting of leisure activities in lived social experience disappears in developed industrial civilizations, because of the development of communications techniques and because in cities or large urbanized zones, the individual is constantly thrown in, especially in his leisure activities, with people who do not belong to the same concrete professional or residential community. A great number of the cultural activities valued by our civilization no longer have their origin in professional activity but in the products of this activity. This change is connected with the most widespread aspect of professional evolution, the firm that produces for a vast market. The individual work is subordinated to the organization of production. Even if one can assure real participation by the workers in the decisions that direct the firm, the fact remains that professionally a very great number of workers or employees perform a task that gives them very little sense of participating in the creation of the finished product. The more techniques progress, the greater the distance between the individual working task and the product. In losing his professional autonomy, the worker has also lost one of the principles of his cultural autonomy. The work of the farmer, the miner, the carpenter gives these workers both satisfaction and dissatisfaction, burdens and sources of pride, that is, a properly professional experience that marks their lives, directly or indirectly, according to whether they are accepted or rejected. The regulated and compartmentalized work of the laborer or employee in the great mechanized organizations, on the other hand, no longer has any properly professional significance for the one who carries it out, and the worker reacts to his work in terms of the economic and social conditions under which he carries it out; in terms of the salary that he draws from it; the social relations, hierarchical or egalitarian, in which it places him; the rhythm in which he must perform it. Coal has no meaning except what the miner's work gives it; land is of no significance without the plow. But the importance of the automobile owes nothing to the work of the assembly-line workers and most often we do not know anything about the men, machines, and plants that produce the goods we seek to acquire and use in our leisure activities and in our entire life.

It may be tempting to oppose active leisure activities to passive leisure activities; these notions have at least the merit of isolating what is new in the present problem, the "passivity" of a great number of leisure activities. Following this line runs the risk of leading to generalizations that are loaded with presuppositions, if one does not at the outset define the meaning of this "passivity." The split between professional activities that have less and less independent meaning for a majority of workers and the cultural activities of the society in which they live must not be presumed but ascertained.

We are witnessing the weakening of cultural expressions bound to a particular social group. Nothing could be clearer than the decline of the traditional "worker culture." Alert educators have replaced the idea of a worker-literature or a worker-culture with the much more realistic and fruitful description of workers participating in the total culture—which may mean participating in a movement of over-all social and political opposition.

What is true on this level of "culture" is true on all the others. Whether it is material or non-material culture, socio-economic groups tend to define themselves more and more by their degree of participation in the activities and products of the culture, and less and less by possession of a subculture different from others. Social roles and cultural roles are more and more separate: categories like neighbor, skilled worker, native of a particular region, no longer explain the television viewer, the reader of the mass circulated paper, the automobile owner.

For the mass of semi-skilled workers, participation in the culture is no longer based on professional life or traditional social role, but on consumption of items and products produced for the entire society. Efforts to redevelop the traditional roots only increases the distance between a man and the culture of the society, only increases his "passivity" in relation to mass leisure activities. Peculiarities are being washed aside and efforts to preserve or remake them are illusory. We must abandon this defensive attitude toward mass culture, for the belief that we can defend the autonomy of social groups against the new centers of cultural influence only supports the traditional class barriers.

Once past this temptation to nostalgia, how do we define leisure activities and how do we support any independence in the face of the increasing influence of the great public or private firms that determine the content and form of the cultural message? Is the greatest activity not also the most complete submission to styles of conduct increasingly engineered from the top of the society?

## Participation and Cultural Withdrawal

At first, the theme of cultural participation seems to answer this concern. Is not cultural underconsumption the lot of those on the bottom rungs of social stratification?

How can one not admit, following Joffre Dumazedier,[1] the importance of simple physical recovery and of elementary social and familial obligations, material and other in a person's life outside of work? On returning from the plant or the office, one must rest, sleep, or relax, and one may have to clear the drain in the sink, stoke the furnace, or put the children to bed. Who could disagree that these obligations partially compensate for needs repressed by work and that they contribute to maintaining the physical and psychological balance of the individual? But the "active" creative value of these semi-leisure activities is limited, at least in the sense that they establish almost no bond between the one who performs them and the cultural values of his society.

Professional compensations—working in one's workshop and other hobbies—probably do not have the importance that some accord to them. On this, Georges Friedmann has made some subtle and disturbing remarks: one's work must possess some professional richness for the worker to seek compensation freely and actively in activities different from his job. Reduced models, like puttering in a workshop, are most often the activities of young men who anticipate that these activities will be of some value in the future. How many unskilled workers with no real trade, and no professional training in school or on the job, seek to create in their free time the substitutes for a professional life and trade that they do not possess? One can only respect them if it testifies to a desire for professional promotion. But is it correct to admire these activities if they mean nothing more than a backward look to a vanished past and if they are a substitute for

[1] Joffre Dumazedier, *Vers une civilisation du loisir* (Paris: Editions du Seuil, 1962).

more positive and active activities? A return to arts and crafts is as fallacious as the "Return to the Land" slogan of sad memory.

In a society of mass production and consumption, activity or passivity depends less on which social group one belongs to and which cultural activities one indulges in than on the degree of social participation. One of the major points of interest in the study of leisure activity is to mark the limits and implications of the idea of social participation. The central idea of an analysis carried out in terms of either cultural participation or withdrawal is that today, when cultural values are attached to mass products, determined by a highly technical civilization with all its social problems, passivity is only the psychological expression of economic and social subjection or dependance.

Certain books and journals sometimes make it seem that only the workers and wage-earners, of all those who are subjected to mass production, live amid a proliferation of leisure activities that numb, condition, and transform them. But we say the contrary and point out the extreme isolation of those with low incomes from the messages of the technical civilization. This is so because, since the production system is so complex and integrated, many workers on the jobs remain in their primary groups and, outside of work, television, newspapers, and magazines penetrate family life without modifying their relationship to the culture in any profound way. The multiplication of spectacles does not transform the spectator into an actor. The mass media do not try to modify attitudes and behavior. Anyway, surveys have shown that their effectiveness in this area is very limited when the ideas are not seconded by groups in which the subject is an active and involved member.

This social "passivity" is connected with the commer-cialization of leisure. In more general terms, it would be more accurate to say that the consumer on the whole has little control over the producer. The only weapon at his disposal is his refusal to consume; but this power is all the weaker as the consumer's attitude becomes more passive—in the case of the movies for example, when he sees more importance in going regularly than in the con-tent of the film. This distance between the consumer and the producer, the consumer's frequent subjection to eco-nomic, moral, and political imperatives that are essentially conservative and mystifying, is the principal problem of a leisure civilization. But these reflections are not addressed to problems of the producer; they simply define the con-sumer's situation. From this point of view, one can sug-gest that the social groups that participate most weakly in sociocultural values are those most passively submissive to mass leisure activities as well as those most attached to family and neighbors, and to either the traditional or to a new type of cultural isolation. There is a connection between the two.

Exposure to mass leisure activities is greater among adolescents than among adults. This striking fact is in-separable from the major social phenomenon of the pro-gressive appearance of adolescence as an autonomous social category in our society. If young workers and em-ployees are not engaged in a really skilled trade, they no longer have to follow a social and professional apprentice-ship. They immediately perform the work that they will carry out for the rest of their lives and often reach their top salary.

These young workers exhibit two principal char-acteristics: intense exposure to the mass media and the

development of an extremely strong informal social
organization. We can refer here to W. F. Whyte's beauti-
ful book, *Street Corner Society,* a study of the social and
cultural life of young men, sons of immigrants, especially
Italians, living in a working-class section of Boston. Both
the good and bad literature on teen-age gangs has shown
to what degree the strengthening of primary social bonds
—whether in accord with or in opposition to the law
makes little difference—is connected with the weak degree
of involvement of these adolescents in the society in which
they live: as marginal individuals (for reasons having to
do with their ethnic background and increasingly also with
their professional futures), they abandon all effort to
achieve broad socialization and content themselves with
a narrow socialization limited to the primary groups to
which they belong. This social and cultural retreat is too
often presented as "criminal"; it is much more often conservative. The evolution of premarital sexual relationships
—dating in the United States, *pololeo* in Latin America—
demonstrates a tendency to the precocious stabilization of
sexual and emotional relations among adolescents; their
behavior approaches that of the adult: in the middle
classes, the seventeen-year-old boy speaks of his girl
and, partly thanks to television, the couple is thus established—whatever may be the degree of development in
terms of the sexual relationship—recognized by parents,
and accepted into the family. Massive consumption of
mechanized leisure activities, far from causing a breakdown of primary social bonds, is actually accompanied by
a precocious development of such bonds. Active participation in primary groups, of friends or neighbors, quasi-
family, is only a compensation for weak social and cultural
activity. Exposure to mass leisure activities is the expres-

sion both of this weak participation and of the desire for greater participation in and contact with situations that open up this closed world of gangs and families.

Membership in primary groups and highly structured communities was the condition for creative participation in social and cultural values in a society in which the culture was a system of meanings directly attached to professional and social experience; now, in a mass civilization, it is only the expression of a forced cultural retreat and a weak participation in the general society.

One comes to the same realization if one considers more broadly the differences in behavior among the social classes. In a recent survey, I was struck with the slight importance of leisure activity in the preoccupations of the workers: in the responses, first, family life and, second, work occupied a greater place. A study carried out in Kansas City and analyzed by Havighurst (in the *American Journal of Sociology* in 1957 and 1959) leads to the same conclusions. The workers appeared more "home-centered" and less "community-centered" than the middle class. The common image of American civilization fits with upper middle-class behavior; social stratification consequently marks differences in participation in community activities that are almost always led by such persons. These "home-centered" persons are not workers attached to a traditional culture based on profession; they are individuals who have neither the financial means nor the social motivations that move the middle class to the foreground of the social scene.

This American study suggests a comparison. In a society both open and conservative, cultural participation is bound to socio-economic levels. But the mass media de-

stroy this traditional bond. Those who are home-centered
—when their home has radio, television, phonographs,
magazines—bypass the social hierarchy of their community to make direct contact with broader social realities
and values. Thus the miner in the north of France, socially
and culturally isolated, establishes, thanks to his television
set, a direct contact with the entire world, far beyond the
traditional forms of social and cultural participation of
the urban middle class.

As soon as we begin to consider a highly evolved industrial civilization in which the traditional professional
and social sources of culture have been in great part
destroyed and in which cultural activity is defined as the
level of participation in values worked out centrally and
no longer on the level of individual lived experience—just
as work is determined by a technical organization and no
longer by the professional experience of the worker—
attachment to cultural values that are bound to one's
trade and primary social groups is no longer an "active"
and creative attitude but rather the expression of weak
participation in the social sources of culture. In this
situation, "passive" submission to the mass media is an
impoverished but positive form of contact with cultural
values. A choice between returning to traditional cultural
themes and memberships or the passive consumption of
the mass media does not exist. These are two closely connected manifestations of cultural underdevelopment,
which is itself bound to the weak participation of the
masses in the values and products of technical civilization
and social democracy. Therefore, we must replace an
analysis that starts from the individual and the psychological functions of leisure activity with a more sociolog-

ical analysis that first of all considers what kind of relations exist within a society, a social class, or an age category, between individuals and the cultural themes that characterize their over-all society.

As we have said, it is indispensable at the outset to sort out leisure activities and to distinguish the various functions that they fulfill. But once this preliminary work is done, it is dangerous to carry on the analysis with the help of ideas that relate purely to individual psychology. Since leisure activities are such a socially and historically defined object of study, it is almost inevitable that the psychological notions used will be full of social presuppositions.

It is not only justifiable but indispensable to inquire into the effects of disjointed piecework on leisure behavior; sociologists and psychologists, psychiatrists and psychoanalysts will work together to great advantage, as the analyses of Erich Fromm and Friedmann demonstrate. But this study of the psychological processes must not be confused with the definition of the situation in which they develop. Unless these two points of view are clearly separated, one risks suggesting that industrial civilization destroys some earlier harmony and balance. While we have said that industrialization ruins the traditional bonds of professional experience, socioprofessional roles, and cultural orientations, we do not think for a moment that pre-industrial societies or those at the beginnings of industrialization are more favorable to cultural initiative.

More practically, it is dangerous to connect the consumption of mass leisure activities too exclusively to piecework, since the workers most directly subject to this kind of work do not seem to be the principal consumers of mass leisure activities. Only on the basis of a sociological definition of the situation under consideration can one profitably utilize notions that refer to individual or even social psychology for the study of behavior that develops in this situation. The expressions *active leisure* and *passive leisure* seem to us dangerous to the degree that they favor the confusion of two analytical levels and insinuate that the passive leisure activities born of modern techniques are opposed to traditional, individual, active leisure activities. They surreptitiously introduce the myth of a harmonious and balanced pre-industrial civilization.

We must go further. Does not the development of mass culture increase freedom of choice by subjecting producers to the increasingly varied tastes of the public instead of cultural values much more closely tied to the established social order? By the same token, it could be reasonably said that the mass production organizations, quite varied and subject to increasingly rapid change, are less restrictive for their members than firms of the old type in which a hierarchized and very concentrated authority limited the influence of the much greater number. The least advanced industrial societies are most authoritarian and bureaucratic. As demands diversify in the cultural order, do not the constraints exercised by the producers become attenuated?

These observations are correct on condition that we add that this freedom of initiative and this capacity to exert influence are progressively more unequally distributed among the various professional and social levels. We must recognize that initiative can only exist at the top of society, while the middle levels are dominated by imitative behavior, and the lower levels by withdrawal or subordination to the spectacles organized by the social elite. In another sense, this reintroduces the distinction between active and passive leisure activities or, if one prefers, between elite and mass culture. This cultural stratification can be somewhat balanced by strong social mobility that dilutes the exclusive influence of background. But this compensation becomes less and less sufficient, for today the upper levels define themselves less by property or money than by education and managerial roles, that is, by cultural characteristics. This creates cultural barriers that are more difficult to breach than economic barriers. Above all, the very existence of mass consumption allows much more potent diffusion of behavior and tastes which strengthen the control of the dominant classes and the ruling groups.

These two series of observations are not contradictory. Mass society on one side appears hierarchized and subjected to increasingly powerful forces of cultural manipulation, and on the other side as a kind of social organization in which the individual's freedom of movement and choice is more and more important so that an increasing number of its members can escape some of the influences exercised over them and can act autonomously. But does this not mean that participation is increasingly dominated and that withdrawal is more and more common and can lead to the formation of new life-styles that are foreign to the mass society, new subcultures to which a rich society permits broad possibilities? Perhaps this is the situation meant by the word *leisure*.

Cultural behavior is determined by both propaganda and social level. But the individual's increasingly specific and limited roles within groups to which he belongs allow long periods for the satisfaction of personal tastes. This permits a certain withdrawal from the constraints of social life. The more the duration of work is reduced the more this area of socially unregulated behavior will be increased. According to the level of one's education and income, it will be dedicated to activities of relaxation or to getting away from social and cultural pressures by escape either in space or time.

The social stratification of leisure activities can be summed up in this way: on the lowest level are those who have the lowest income and remain locked into marginal zones marked by the decay of earlier cultural worlds—immigrant workers from culturally different countries or regions, workers in declining industries, the aged, low-scale wage-earners who try to protect themselves by maintaining family bonds. Above them, there is the large number of production workers who do not participate in the mass culture except by their acquisition of products and their consumption of spectacles and who protect themselves by withdrawal into primary groups. Above them, there are those whose work is defined by a function and rank in an organization. This group is the most open to the influence of clearly hierarchized cultural messages. For this group, promotion, mobility, and the imitation of the higher groups are essential objectives. Finally, at the top, those who perform tasks connected with management or knowledge and have no great "status anxiety" cultivate an aristocratic style of life: cultural activity for its own sake, freedom to move in time and space, an interest in searching for new cultural experiences.

This quick sketch shows at least that the convenient expression *mass culture* means neither the equalization of cultural consumption nor the formation of a universe of leisure activity independent from professional activity. Like leisure activities, consumer activities are more and

more socially labeled; innovation is increasingly concentrated at the top. This cultural integration is not
necessarily restrictive. It becomes so only if a strongly
centralized political power acting according to an explicit
ideology governs all cultural production. When this is
not the case, an increasing number of individuals have
the possibility of withdrawal, escape, or autonomous
choice, that is, they can form new elective groups. This
constitutes the essence of what we call leisure and is why,
in rich societies, individuals who are questioned generally
feel themselves "free." But the essential fact is that cultural
activity is determined by the level of social participation,
by the place occupied on the ladder of stratification.

This lends itself to a very classic insight. Those with
weak professional, economic, and social participation are
turned in on primary groups based on kinship, neighborhood, or work, and view the broader society as a spectacle
brought into their homes by words and pictures. More
active leisure activities develop to the degree that the
level of social participation is raised, which quite simply
reflects the conclusion of the statisticians: to the degree
that the standard of living is raised, the portion of the
budget that can be used for elective, personalized activities that are relatively liberated from the needs of
elementary subsistence increases more than propor-
tionately.

Having criticized the illusion of a return to active
leisure activities rooted in a particular social experience,
we must now step back from the theme of social participation and ask whether it may not lead to consequences opposed to those too generously assigned it.

## *Cultural Demands*

If we avoid the temptation to respond to a new situation with the artificial reinforcement of an old type of direct bond between an individual and his social group and culture, or the specific subculture of a socioprofessional situation, we must inquire into the new nature of the bond between individuals and their culture in highly evolved industrial societies. Up to this point, we have met ambiguous expressions of this relationship and we must now separate more distinctly its implications. The breaking of the bonds between cultural activities and membership in real social groups can lead in two directions. On one side, one can say that "active" leisure activities are bound to a higher degree of social participation which is defined by high income or by having at one's disposition the greatest number of collective cultural instruments. On the other side, one can take a more radical approach and suggest that cultural activity is bound to an increasingly complete "desocialization" of the culture. We shall try to follow this second approach which will show that broadened social participation, far from favoring cultural initiatives, only reinforces social integration and stratification and, consequently, cultural inequalities and imitative behavior.

We must begin from the nature of the cultural models in our society. When we affirm that new cultural values are formed on the level of the products of activity more than on the level of the activity itself, we are forced to add that the new cultural models define situations more than behavior. Science, technical progress, overcoming distance by mass information, speed, or jets, performances achieved by instruments, machines, or the human body are all cultural themes organized around notions of progress, domination, and control of natural conditions that involve no rule of social conduct. Many saddened observers have seen in this a decline of "moral values," an expression of Promethean pride, a Faustian madness. These reactions (stripped of their ideological content which is unimportant here) have the merit (as do those of their more optimistic adversaries) of insisting on the *amoral* and *asocial* character of the new cultural values. Without this realization, one cannot understand the importance of the problem of leisure activities, for they constitute, at least apparently, a leap beyond the rules that govern moral and social life or, depending on the tone one prefers to adopt, either a flight from obligations or a liberation from constraints.

This leads us to criticize another of the expressions that we have ourselves used: mass leisure activities. For if the means by which culture is diffused are massive, the cultural experience, the contact with cultural themes, is more individualized than formerly, since the mass of the participants are often, and increasingly, only a mass in the abstract as moviegoers or television viewers but actually isolated from each other by the walls of their homes or the darkness of the theaters.

The example of the cinema helps us to move beyond this superficial statement, for the cinema must both be realistic, as S. Kracauer says, showing wretchedness, war, love, and the human countenance as they are and, at the same time, it exists only by arousing in the viewers mechanisms of projection and identification, to follow the central theme of Edgar Morin. This union of the real world and the imaginary man—never better achieved than in the cinematic image *par excellence,* the enlarged face of the hero or star—defines the double nature of the mass media.

The counterpart of the amorality of the themes is the creation by the participants themselves of conscious or unconscious attitudes, constantly innovative and changing, free personal interpretations of cultural themes which are objectives more than models. This is the sense in which we must understand the increasing *technicity* of leisure activities. It is true that technique itself is one of the most important cultural values in our society. But technicity plays a wider role by changing the nature of the contact between the individual and a great number of cultural values.

This technicity eliminates all normative approaches to the degree that they traditionally imply a certain code of conduct. A purely technical conception of art may, for example, neglect the meaning of the work of art; but this danger is largely compensated for by the revolutionary worth of this "abstraction" that leaves each individual free to commit his whole personality to the activity or the cultural contact. The absence of "objective" meaning in many aspects of the culture allows each to establish between the element of the culture and himself a direct, personal, and partly incommunicable, bond. Let us take the example of dance: a folk dance, most often a group dance, defines each one's role morally and socially. Such a dance possesses a theme that defines each participant's situation and feelings, particularly in types of love relationships. To the degree that the couple becomes one agent, the definition of social roles is removed and the role of personal interpretation increases. Nevertheless, a waltz or tango still imposes certain sentiments on the participants. On the other hand, the sometimes spectacular importance of technique in contemporary dances allows the dancers total liberty not only on the level of improvisation (in which the dance achieves the freedom of a "jam session") but especially on the level of relations between the partners. Technique appears to be the necessary condition for liberation from rules and laws; technique does not express sentiments, it frees them from social and moral conventions and establishes a clear but secret relation between the partners.

Everyone senses that this example has importance only because it evokes love. Only today is there finally taking place a generalization of the great theme that came from Renaissance Italy, eighteenth-century France, and D. H. Lawrence—pleasure-love, that is, leisure-love, freed from its social constraints and its moral rules. Who would argue that those who recall that love is *made* and has its own techniques are reducing it to gestures? The impersonality of its rules is only the mask of modesty and secrecy that covers the encounter of two persons.

This freedom from rules and from accepted or socially imposed models of behavior is the true measure of the existence of leisure activities. Materially, free time has been developed at the expense of working time, both in terms of the week and of standards of living. Even more important progress has been made in terms of free activity, the passage from culture to leisure and more specially from folklore to leisure activity. This change is so profound that the term *leisure activity,* as useful and revealing as it is, sometimes seems insufficient. It would be preferable to speak of deliberate, unregulated behavior.

Those facets of cultural life that are farthest from leisure activities in the ordinary sense of the word evidence the same cultural change that is characteristic of our time. It will suffice to raise the example of religious life: its evolution is analogous to that of dance in the example that we have just raised.

The most elementary analysis of religious behavior can distinguish at least three different meanings. There is first what we can call traditional religion—recognizing the great inexactnes of this term—the dependence and submission of man relative to an order that is both natural and supernatural to which one must conform, a kind of religion in which rites and obligations play a central role. Secondly, there is membership in a church or sect, that is, in a social organization that is strongly bound to the surrounding society. The simplest of such bonds is the correspondence between religious affiliation or roles and social stratification: the black who has come to Chicago gradually climbs the hierarchy of churches as he grows more prosperous and moves from the north to the south of the black section. Finally, there is religion as the apprehension of human destiny, existence, and death. In Western society, de-Christianization, the crumbling or collapse of Christian society, has reduced the importance of the first two aspects of religious life and, if it does not increase, at least it isolates the importance of the third. I suggest that the historic importance of "progressive" Christianity does not result from the fact that it tries to transform the role of social allegiance of the Catholic—or Protestant—Church as much as from the fact that it critically cuts the traditional lines of religious life and opens the way to autonomous religious behavior. Like the dance and painting, religion becomes a leisure activity, that is, deliberate, unregulated behavior, personal and secret: the priest-worker is not externally different from those with whom he works; he is not protected by a collection of outward rules of behavior; he simply gives his life a different meaning. The Christian and the non-Christian no longer live in different societies and moral worlds; they simply live different experiences.

In thus relating leisure activity and religion, our intention is not to equate religious life with movies or bowling, but to recognize in all the aspects of culture the same general evolution that casts light on the profound meaning of leisure activity: the passage from socially and morally regulated behavior to action freely oriented toward objects or values that are all the more demanding of the individual to the degree that they are no longer separated from him by a labyrinth of social codes.

This transformation of cultural activities comes into conflict with some contrary tendencies. It can be viewed as a reinforcement of social participation and integration in two main ways. First, the struggle against the influence of commercialized consumption may lead to a collective organization of leisure activities and to the development of collective instruments through which social integration is achieved. Second, mass consumption may lead to an increasingly precise stratification, the diversity of life-styles being replaced by the hierarchy of living standards and the segregation of different styles of consumption. We must pause over these tendencies that are destructive to leisure activities.

In the first place, it is possible to admit our criticism of "cultural withdrawal," and yet to interpret it in a different sense from ours: if it is true, one may say, that the cultural themes of our society are less bound than formerly to professional activity and to the particular social experience of individuals and more to products and situations born of the activity of the collectivity, the bond between the culture and the society must be created and maintained by the collectivity itself and individuals must be put in contact with cultural values by means of collective instruments. If the era of cultural particularism is over, that of the organized participation of all in the common culture is beginning.

This collectivist position is quite naturally opposed by the liberalism of the rich countries in which the development of living standards, the diffusion of education and of the means of information theoretically permit all to reach all the material and non-material products of the culture. This simple opposition is nevertheless false, for it willfully confuses cultural activity with the institutional conditions that allow individuals to have contact with the products of the culture.

In stressing the individualization of cultural activity, we have touched only the first of these problems. It is possible to defend at the same time the idea of a socialization of cultural activities, if only to criticize their commercialization in a society like ours; but this political position has no right to declare that access to cultural goods is necessarily bound to more rigid social integration and must be accompanied by universal adoption of certain behavior models.

If one accepts our preceding analyses, such a position signifies the disappearance of the fundamental meaning of leisure activities, that is, the individual's freedom of behavior when he participates in certain cultural objectives. Soviet society considers antisocial and reactionary every effort to realize, either nobly or poorly, this freedom of the individual relative to his own culture and society. From this results its moral and aesthetic rigorism and the decisive role of the State in the formulation of moral, aesthetic, and intellectual judgments to which all must submit.

This denial of leisure activities, their reduction to a regulated mechanism for the assimilation of social and cultural norms, is a present danger in all efforts to define and impose a lay morality, socialist realism, or an absolute science of man and society. Each advance of social democracy in France sees an often open conflict develop between the two conditions necessary for the existence of a "popular culture": by confusing the end with the means, attachment to political means to democratize the culture risks giving birth to cultural dogmatism. Simultaneously, the development of leisure activities brings about a sudden individualization of leisure behavior that seems to weaken, to "bourgeoisize," the political and social pressure thanks to which the access of all to leisure activity and culture has been made possible.

For the foreseeable future, conflicts will be built into the necessary union between organized social action—both enriched and burdened by its organization and the power of its objectives, utopias, and myths—and the individual enjoyment of the cultural areas already won by collective struggle. Do all who advocate the democratization of leisure accept its necessary consequence: the end of any correspondence between social organization and cultural values, the withering away of the central role of social groups in the orientation of cultural behavior?

Let us now turn to the other side. Does mass culture lead to a breakdown of the stratification of cultural behavior, or, on the contrary, to new forms of social hierarchization? The destruction of particular life-styles does not bring about an equality in levels of social participation. On the contrary, the social hierarchy is defined much more clearly once it is no longer hidden behind the multiplicity of life-styles. The unification of the cultural market makes it more and more dependent on those with the greatest purchasing power or influence. To the degree that social mobility increases in a society, the diffusion of cultural models and the concentration of the power to spread them also increase. In a parallel way, social stratification becomes more marked and the individual is defined by his level in the scale. His cultural behavior comes to depend increasingly on others' judgment of his level. Cultural initiative is concentrated on the higher levels.

It is appropriate to add an important observation to this summary of the analyses already presented. To this reinforcement of social stratification is added the increasing importance of segregation. First of all, material segregation: income levels are more and more clearly differentiated in urban space. Even more important, social segregation: each group defends its own level by avoiding the marginal elements that threaten to lower it, for example, by lowering property values.

More precisely, if a social group can no longer be defined by a particular cultural content, it seeks all the more actively to isolate itself from other groups whose practice is less and less different from its own but which are not on the same social level. To the degree that traditional barriers fall, other more elective barriers are raised. The decline of cultural discrimination gives rise to the increase of segregation. Clubs, associations, youth movements, or unions can be used in this way. It is remarkable that these social barriers have a purely negative role: they do not—as the barriers formerly raised by local and professional communities did—protect certain specific activities of these communities; they aim only at isolating certain social groups in their practice of activities which are no longer special to them. There is more than money behind such barriers. Viennese social democracy after World War I was set up as a society within society: one played chess, billiards, cards in social-democratic clubs. Likewise, the members of the Komsomol tend to isolate themselves from others. Accordingly, we ascertain a social stratification in the practice of leisure activities at the same time as there is a destratification of the leisure activities themselves. Greater homogeneity of the content of the activities is accompanied by a setting-up of partitions in the social forms they take.

These remarks lead directly to a more general formulation. The breakdown of the traditional bonds between cultural activities and particular social collectivities opens the way to two opposed processes. The first gives rise to what is called mass society and mass culture. This makes cultural activities attributes of social function and social level; it makes them products to be consumed. As de Jouvenel has wisely recalled, this democracy of mass consumption rests on the principle of the inequal vote. Not only do the rich vote, that is, buy, more often than others but, since living costs absorb a much smaller part of their income, they enjoy a quasi-monopoly over the creation of consumable goods and services. Cultural activity is subjected to social stratification and also to the forms in which work is organized. The social organization of space, when it leads to segregation according to income levels, increases the influence of social integration. For their part, the large firms, especially when located outside metropolitan centers, constitute hierarchized social and cultural milieux.

This mass society strengthens the influence of the areas of primary socialization, especially the family. Cultural instruments within the home, neighborhood relations, and voluntary local associations reinforce social and cultural distance, and educate children in strongly differentiated worlds. This recalls some of the best-known themes of David Riesman. It is unnecessary to repeat here how futile it would be to oppose to this stratified society the nostalgic dream of a community and to imagine a metropolis both rich in the stimulations of the mass society in which there would also be the forms of generalized participation of a small pre-industrial city or of one of those lower-class neighborhoods so beloved by snobs.

Let us recall again that this social integration of cultural activities can take forms other than mass consumption. It can be achieved by administrative means rather than by commercial means. The collective arrangements that the communist municipalities in the worker sections outside Paris have often set up in a remarkable manner are also means to achieve a high degree of integration. Their advantage is that they counteract the influences that lead to imitation; their weakness is that they enclose the consumer on a middle level, where he is deprived of creativity. The social framework built around leisure activities in Soviet-type countries most often strengthens social mobility by placing emphasis on instruction, professional advancement, and political participation and, at the same time, establishes an extreme cultural conservatism that multiplies conservatories of culture rather than centers of innovation. The commercial and administrative variants of social integration are assuredly very different from one another but each gives absolute priority to integration and to reinforcement of the social hierarchy.

The other possible direction "desocializes" cultural activities. It more directly relates a cultural model based on scientific and technical knowledge, hence on systems of formalization rather than ideas and socio-moral contents, with a defense or affirmation of personal existence. Because our society is oriented by knowledge and development, that is, because it is technical, the individual—defined by his own personality outside of his professional and social roles—articulates new demands instead of being governed by a specific image of man, society, and the world.

Education is less and less defined as socialization, that is, as an apprenticeship for social roles. On one side, it is the learning of languages; on the other, it is the discovery and formation of personality. These two orientations are in constant tension but they are not contradictory. They both bypass the organization of the social hierarchy: one by going over it through cultural models, the other by going under it through the autonomy of personality. A contemporary industrial society possesses cultural creativity to the degree that it counters the control of stratified consumption by establishing an alliance between individuality and cultural models that are increasingly free of any particular social content.

Cultural activity is opposed to social organization. Science and individuality are allied against integration in massive organizations and against the stratification of life styles. Culture is affirmed as the creation of a "state of nature," according to Serge Moscovici,[2] that is, as the con-

[2] Serge Moscovici, *Essai sur l'histoire humaine de la nature* (Paris: Flammarion, 1968).

struction of a relation between man and his material, physical, and biological environment. We must reject the superficial opposition between work and leisure and replace it with the opposition between culture and social organization.

In a society of mass production and consumption, there cannot be radical separation between work activities and activities outside work. The forces that dominate society do not any longer exercise their influence only within firms; whatever these forces may be, they extend their control to the whole of economic and social life, to consumption as well as to the organization of space and education. Consumption as well as professional activity defines one's place in a hierarchized social system.

In a different way, however, creative activity is not to be identified with the organization of work. The researcher is not an executive. Scientific discovery is not the management of the firm; the language of mathematics is not that of the bureaucracy. Likewise, hierarchized consumption is not identified with the affirmation of the individual.

In the second part of this essay, we showed that "mass culture" had two complementary aspects: stratification of consumption and hierarchization of the forms of personal autonomy. There is no apparent split between these observations and the new propositions that we have just introduced in insisting on both the importance of abstract cultural models and the importance of private life in our kind of society. Yet there is profound opposition between these two representations. In the first case, cultural behavior is embodied in social stratification; in the second, it transcends it in terms of both cultural models and personal "needs."

This is why the role of youth, especially students, is so

important in cultural demands. They are the group least integrated into the social organization and stratification, the group most attracted by the new forms of knowledge and most involved in the problems of personal life. While mass culture reconciles and controls the two poles of our cultural system by subjecting them to the framework of social organization, cultural demands appeal to creativity against participation, bear witness to the conflict between knowledge and personal life and the opposition between cultural initiative and social organization.

Enough has been said about youth and its participation in the mass culture to recall here that in separating cultural activity from social participation one is also thinking of the situation of the elderly. Their marginality is hopeless if the only operative principle is the virtues of social participation. Their degree of participation is necessarily slight; they no longer have professional activity, their income is low, their capacity for participation in a society of rapid cultural changes is diminished. Everyone knows that no advance is made in solving this problem by dreaming of communities of the elderly, or clubs for the retired. The life of the elderly can be enhanced only if old age—like youth—is recognized as a particular experience, as the time of free activities and not of social participation, as the time for memory and imagination rather than retreat. Above all, does not the consciousness of the body at this age best unify participation in scientific knowledge and personal experience? I realize that these are cursory observations, but they indicate a general direction for reflection, for our societies will be marked by a growing number of individuals able to participate only weakly in society: the retired, the ill, and the handicapped. If we measure them only according to their degree of participation, they will remain nothing but marginal individuals. This reasoning, hidden under the silent acquiescence of the majority, accepts the reintroduction of wretchedness at the very moment when progress in productivity tends to diminish its importance in the world of work.

The privatization of culture that we are discussing can only be creative if it is bound to participation in the cultural objectives that define the historicity of our society: knowledge, the systems of formalization, the transformation of the universe. This can come about only through the reconciliation of two processes.

First, cultural models and languages must be massively diffused and placed at the center of society, not at its summit. This is the setting in which the problems of education and the city must be posed. In both cases, it is a matter of desocializing the cultural models that are proposed, of weakening the role of heritage and of "content." Far from seeking to recreate generalized participation in sociocultural "values," technicocultural models must be diffused and bound to the demands of personality. Art plays this role to the degree that it associates formalization and imagination, that it is "dehumanized," that is, it becomes language and desire instead of message and representation of society and its sentiments. The city is a place of exchange and consumption, but it can also be a work of art—not a place in which works of art are enclosed but a union of artistic constructions and imaginative appeal, a natural rather than a social place, where matter and formalizations are associated.

This image of the city is the opposite of the urban community that is frequently opposed to the cities whose growth has been bound to industrialization. Its basis is not the search for social integration and participation but the complementarity and separation of centers of cultural influence from the spaces of personal life. These would occupy a dispersed habitat in which "nature" was mixed with a flexible urban pattern. This clearly supposes considerable development of individual and collective means of transportation. This tendency is evident in most metropolitan centers, where the inner city is empty and the old sections are either disorganized or are reoccupied by a new aristocracy ready to pay dearly for proximity to the centers of cultural influence and consumption of the past. The majority of the population is scattered in more and more distant suburbs; the separation of dwelling-place from working-place becomes an increasingly costly problem to resolve but it is one of the economic costs of a new organization of space, just as the management of land supposes important investments in all kinds of communications.

Secondly, beyond this coexistence there must be cultural criticism of socialized consumption. If leisure is not to be only a matter of consumption, it must be demanding and critical. This is why there is so much talk of cultural revolt and opposition to the mass society and social integration. This is why the opposition movement unites scientists, artists, and the young against the forces of social integration and cultural manipulation.

Grievances and demands must be directed first against the reduction of personal life to the desire to consume, to please, and to succeed, embellished often with illusions of "self-expression." Commercialized eroticism and fashion are two of the ambiguous areas in which profound cultural innovations that often transform one's relationship to the body are "recuperated" by the hierarchized world of consumerism and money. This example shows that to oppose mass culture to cultural criticism as if they were entirely separate areas would make the latter merely the defense of traditional or aristocratic models. They actually represent opposed "policies" which orient the dissolution of former cultural forms in different directions.

Nothing is more superficial than a global condemnation of mass culture and its content. One must oppose to this rejection a critical attitude that frees cultural innovation from the social control that weighs it down. Just as in the last century some totally rejected industrialization, only criticism of its social control and of the uses to which it was put led to the formation of social movements and social change. Cultural demands must also be directed against the social utilization of scientific knowledge; if they reject this type of knowledge in order to prefer ideology or emotionalism, they become sectarian. But they will be effective when they question the alliance between knowledge and the social order, especially the confusion of intellectual competence with the power to make decisions in the university itself. This cultural demand is creative only if it is "untamed," only if it does not become the tool of new forces of social integration. When one opposes high culture (considered as liberating) to the mass media, this is only the defense of an aristocratic conception of society which reinforces a hierarchized style of consumption. When one opposes the organization of leisure activities to free time, one is only proposing a different form of social integration—as oppressive, and sometimes more so.

The techniques of cultural diffusion permit—at least to the degree that they are not regulated by the political and administrative authorities—the expression of the imagination and the demands of the personality. Sociocultural opposition fights against the control of consumption. Education and scientific instruction allow the greatest number to participate in the new cultural models. It is evident that the liberation of the individual, political activity, and scientific creation cannot be associated without crisis and tension. But this is the coalition that opposes the constraints of the massive organizations and stratified consumption.

In this way, we define oppositions and conflicts that do not correspond to those most often presented. Many have rejected Bergson's call for an increase of soul in different ways. Indeed, our societies need less soul, less morality, and fewer values. These great words too easily conceal the control of political power and ruling classes. Our societies need an increase of body and an increase of science. They need to rediscover—counter to the pressures exercised by all the structures and stratifications—the demands and creativity of the individual as well as the internal demands of knowledge and its languages.

This conclusion is less ideological than it appears. It is easy to add that no society can function without organization, stratification, and mechanisms for social integration. For a sociologist to pose the problem of leisure activity is not to appeal to man and his spontaneity against society and its constraints, but to reveal the opposition between the social order and its instruments of integration on one hand and the forces of scientific invention and personal education on the other. What must be broken open is the false unity of what is called mass consumption instead of considering it as a real whole that some accept and others reject. The sociology of leisure activity is the study of the conflicts between social integration and cultural creation.

# POSTSCRIPT

# Why Sociologists?

We have defined some of the aspects of the new society that is gradually being organized around us. At this point, another question arises: Can the economist or the sociologist accurately define the changes a society is undergoing, if that society is itself not actively involved with these changes through debates, conflicts, and political adjustments? Was it possible to analyze capitalist society in depth before the worker struggles began, before political life was transformed and ideologies and utopias appeared?

After having been absorbed for a long time by the problems of its own economic reconstruction, by the divisions in Europe and the bloody resistance to the independence movements of the colonized peoples, French society has gradually become conscious of the exigencies and difficulties inherent in economic growth. Until very recently, it had not experienced, either in ideas or actions, the conflicts raised by this growth; one result was the weakness of sociological analysis. Sociology hesitated indecisively between an ideology that reduced all social problems to resistance to necessary and self-justified change and recourse to notions inherited from an earlier situation. The progress of sociological analysis is not simply a matter of developing studies or working out new concepts. It supposes that society will react to its own changes, that it will define objectives and experience the social and cultural conflicts through which the direction of the changes and the form of the new society may be debated. If the theme that runs through the preceding chapters, the birth of a new type of society, the programmed society, meets such strong resistance, is it not because French society is passively undergoing its changes rather than living them out voluntarily in the midst of hope and conflict?

Blinded by the vigor of economic growth and the rapidity of social change, sociology has often refused to define the new society that is being formed out of economic, social, and cultural change. Whether it limits itself to studying the conditions for effectively adapting individuals and groups to change, or sticks to noting the continuance of older forms of economic power, cultural inequalities, and social conflicts, it turns away from the research into new determinants of growth, new social classes, new struggles, and new models of social and cultural action. The chapters of this book are a protest against a sociological "empiricism" that cloaks the meaning of historic changes with counterfeit clarity by appealing to change, modernization, or the mass society and concentrates all its attention on the responses of individuals and groups to a new situation. What we need most urgently is not an analysis of social behavior but of society, considered no longer as a situation bct as a system of action, a network of cultural orientations and power relationships.

If French sociology hesitates to commit itself to this path, a large part of the reason is that French society is not "making" its own history. The exhaustion of the Jacobin model of action has often been denounced but almost always in the name of a neo-liberal pragmatism that speaks only of adaptation, flexibility, and strategy. Until the spring of 1968, French society had not been dominated by any great social and political debate. This does not mean that it is permanently free of social struggles and ideologies. In fact, it is dominated by the reign of the Whigs, that is, the combination of the old and new ruling classes under the protection of a State that is both powerful and stifling, modern and conservative.

In this sense, we can speak of depoliticization, which does not mean indifference on the part of the electorate or the disappearance of choices or conflicts. The political parties defend the interests of certain social groups, seek to direct the State, and sometimes relate themselves to over-all conceptions of political power and the social regime. But they are hardly at all vivified by any questioning of political power. Politics seems trapped on the level of institutions. It does not question the ruling powers whose authority governs the functioning of the institutions. Very often, political sentiment must become involved with faraway problems before it can take form.

We have political institutions; some of them wish to create new power; others wish to combat it. But political sentiments and the institutions almost never come into contact. Political thought is undisciplined, outside the institutions. Political problems have been posed only through revolt, primarily that of the students, almost all of whom stand outside of political organizations. As a social movement and a cultural uprising, the May Movement was not a properly political force defined by a program, an organization, and a strategy. In an undisciplined way, it revealed contradictions: it had neither the will nor the capacity to further the institutionalization of the conflicts that it triggered. Its importance is due to the fact that it restored to French society the consciousness of its historicity; that it questioned power and class relations; that it raised up ideologies and utopias; that it imposed the realization that a society is not only the collection of the means and effects of economic growth but primarily the confrontation between the forces that struggle for the control of change and for the creation of antagonistic models of development.

The analysis of contemporary society can only be ideological so long as such social movements do not recreate a practice of historicity which sociology can then study, describe, and explain. But sociological explanation, paralyzed when it precedes the social action that reveals its object to it, must never merely reproduce the consciousness of the participants in the action and confuse their statements with its own work.

The essays gathered in this book testify more to the intention than to the results of sociological analysis. They each try to relate to the social movements whose action alone justifies their existence. They also try to keep a distance from the participants and their ideologies. In this sense, our effort is analogous to that which is pursued, under difficult and uncertain conditions, in the teaching of sociology. Only the social commitment of the students can transform the analytical efforts of the teachers. It is the teachers' role to constantly reinforce the internal demands of knowledge, to replace ideology with explanation, passion with reason. This is difficult today when the new social movements are turned inward on the universities and political intentions weigh (by definition) too heavily on the highly specific activity of intellectual analysis.

But this difficulty must absolutely not be allowed to send us back to approaches that seem better protected from dangerous contamination. This would be the complete triumph of ideology because it would preclude the debates and struggles that define the historic existence of a society. French society is changing, certainly. But toward what, led by whom, and at what price?

In my opinion, sociology has never been in a more favorable position. The definition of the fundamental mechanisms of social evolution used to be assigned to strictly economic analysis; today growth and change can only be conceived as the result of social processes. Problems of power used to be identified with those of the State and the analysis of political facts was an area quite separated from sociology. Today, the close relationship and even confusion between power and institutions is tending to disappear. Institutions are coming to be seen as spheres of social meaning, while power is ceasing to be identified with personages. Pagès has introduced the notion of hold (*emprise*) which seems to insist primarily on the impersonal character of a power that shows itself not so much through decisions as by the almost natural "logic" of styles of organization, production, and decision-making. It is defined more by its capacity to impede the social indictment, hence the social control, of the instruments of change than by the imposition of a sovereign will. The sphere of sociological analysis grows to the degree that society's capacity to act on itself increases.

It is true that today the explosion of contestation seems about to break apart this sphere of analysis, with techno-cratic voluntarism on one side, and on the other the passionate rejection of what it conceals. The sociologist is subjected to opposing pressures from these contrary utopias. Overly complacent references to the May uprising must not help French society to free itself from the need for historic action. It is not enough to rebel against a society that has been reduced to the economy on one side and to personal power on the other; it is not enough to define the objectives and methods of possible political action; one must recognize first of all that French society, like most European societies, is having more and more trouble existing on the level of historic action. If it ever becomes incapable of doing so, or above all if it renounces the attempt to do so, I strongly doubt that sociology will be able to find any reason for existing or the ability to recognize its great problems.

During recent years, society has been slumbering in prosperity and growth. Today, after the social and political wrenching of May '68, the risk is that it may reject problems that seem insoluble and gradually grow accustomed to recognizing an untamed area outside the governable, programmed areas. If this rejection of opposition comes about, society will see its capacity to act on itself disappear and it will be unable to avoid falling into dependence. Sociology will then be only the bad conscience of society.

Is this not one more reason for affirming the necessity of sociology, a necessity that is not only intellectual but personal? Only sociology makes it possible to transcend the contradictions between the impersonal control exercised by technocracy and the revolt in the name of personal and collective creativity. Only sociology can rediscover the political reality of our society and evoke the social power behind the impersonal control and the social movements behind the revolt.

The intellectual problem facing the sociologist is the political problem that faces the society: how to transform into development and conflictual participation in social change the indispensable and unavoidable direct confrontation between control and revolt. Sociology can no longer oppose to social constraints the exigencies and moral values embodied in an idea of Man, nor content itself with describing each element of social practice as if it could be understood independently of the place it occupies within a field of historic action. For too long sociology has gone along beside changes that took place here and there. The political reawakening of the society that it studies, or at least the questioning of its directions and the forms of its organization, allows the sociologist to rediscover the unity of the object of his study and of his own work.

# Index

Born in 1925, former professor of sociology at Nanterre, director of the Laboratory of Industrial Sociology at Ecole Pratique des Hautes Etudes, ALAIN TOURAINE has taught at Columbia University and at U.C.L.A. and in South America. He is the author of *The May Movement: Revolt and Reform,* and other volumes and critical articles. He is past president of the French Sociological Association.